The greatest promise ever made

RAPTURE

?

by

Walt Chaney

CITIOFBOOKS, INC.
3736 Eubank NE Suite A1
Albuquerque, NM 87111-3579
www.citiofbooks.com

Hotline: 1 (877) 389-2759
Fax: 1 (505) 930-7244

Ordering Information:
Quantity sales. Special discounts are available on quantity purchases by corporations, associations, and others. For details, contact the publisher at the address above.

Printed in the United States of America.

ISBN-13:   Paperback   979-8-89391-350-7
            eBook   979-8-89391-351-4

Library of Congress Control Number: 2024919766

Table of Contents

CHAPTER 1
RELIGIOUS REDMAN

In a small, rural county in central Virginia, not much was happening…ever. Sure, there were the usual weddings followed by the week-long honeymoons at some nearby place or the occasional misfortune when one of the local boys tried blowing up a beer can with an M-80 while holding it between his knees. Other than that, exciting moments such as those, life was pretty laid back and dysfunctional in Bumpass Virginia.

For high-school seniors like Wally and his pals, Dalton and Ed and along with a few others, the overwhelming desire was to escape to—either to some local college or to one of Uncle Sam's fearless fighting forces where they could shoot A-rabs or some other species of terrorists that they had heard about, anything was better than shooting road signs and beating roadside mailboxes into submission with baseball bats. They searched for anything better than having a sore butt every Sunday from sitting for two-plus hours listening to the divinely inspired rantings of the local preacher and the echoing *"Amens"* from the blindly devoted congregation at the Holier Than Thou Pentecostal Church as they watched the church varsity serpent-handlers risk certain death by playing with venomous copperheads and rattlers.

So again, in that small, rural county in central Virginia, not much was happening…ever…, yet a mysterious aura of change was in the air.

"Mama, I don't wanna go to church," whined Wally, "those people are crazy! I ain't see no need to go to church."

"Now, Wally, you know they're crazy about the Lord. Pastor Zeb is full of the Holy Spirit, and he only wants to share the Holy Spirit." Wally's mother, a God-fearing Christian woman. Responded with genuine enthusiasm. Her five foot four frame was the shape of a pear. Red hair with freckles adorned her complexion and when she smiled her blue eyes widen. Wally looked into her eyes and knew she was sincere about her faith and devotion to the Lord. She of all people made the existence and reliance on God, real.

"Pastor Zeb proves it every Sunday!" interjected Malachi, Wally's father, in an assertive tone, as he stared Wally down with his yellowish, red-veined eyes, as tobacco juice slid from his lip. As always, his firm, evil stare frightened Wally who cowered under his father's response.

Mumbling under his breath, Wally turned his thoughts toward Jesus and quoted *Matthew 4, ⁵ Then the devil took him to the holy city and had him stand on the highest point of the temple. ⁶ "If you are the Son of God," he said, "throw yourself down."*

"Wally, you're a heathen! You're deceived by the master of lies! That old demon wants to steal your very soul, and besides that is not what that verse means!! Oh Lord, have mercy on this precious child; he does know what he says! Today, Wally, you might speak in tongues for the first time. Once you receive the Holy Ghost, you will feel different about your faith and devotion to Christ our Lord. That will change everything!" his mother whispered.

"Booya! I'll slap yerr mouth! Now get'in the dern truck!" Malachi in his stained white dress shirt hollered from the front porch of the ninety-foot, double-wide trailer that had been inherited from Wally's grandfather. He spit over the wobbly paint peeling railing.

As Wally sat squeezed between his portly parents, he wondered what life would be like outside of his rural town in Virginia. He thought to himself, *"I can't wait to get to Virginia Tech!"* He had just received his letter of acceptance into the biology department at that large university. His thoughts continued: *"God, what does my future hold? Do you hold it in your hands? I need a sign!"*

Their old rusty Ford truck lumbered through the rural countryside, finally crossing a narrow covered wooden bridge. On the other end of the bridge, the white church steeple rose against the green Appalachian ridgeline. Malachi pulled into the sparsely graveled, red-mud parking lot, past the sign at the entry to that welcomed parishioners to the *Holier than Thou Pentecostal Church in Bumpass*.

"Come on boy, it's the first Sunday of the month. Let's get it ready." After completing the task ordered by his father, Wally stepped out the back door of the church.

He mumbled, "That should keep the old man happy until lunch time." Completing the task ordered by his father, Wally made it to the pulpit area and placed the communion supplies for the ushers. He hurried to the back of the church and as he passed the back door to the baptizing pool, he heard a small commotion. Deacon Connard was fixing his bow tie as he opened the rear stage door. Wally knew he had a reputation with the ladies and figured he witnessed some hanky-panky before the service. Wally looked up at the blushed face man and moved quickly past him. Wally moved his head side to side. He thought to himself, *"inside the church, fornication."* Without the fear of a consequence, because adultery would be the topic of the church congregation for years. "Hey Brother, that's a commandment and you better tie that bow a little tighter, your foreskin goin cover your face. He chuckled as he walked away. In a very guilty defensive response, Deacon Connard said hatefully, "you little…"

"Oh, by the way where did you learn to back up a car? Ya better stop popping over the curb in the rear lot. You're going break the curb. Hey Connard don't ya know those curbs are there for a reason." Wally laughed as he started skipping out the rear door.

He stepped out the back door and saw Dalton and Ed arriving in Dalton's lifted, rebuilt 2006 Tacoma in the parking lot. Wally walked toward the boys. "Durn Mom and Dad woke me up to go to church. Geez, next year while in the Airforce, I'm sleepin in Sunday mornings announced Ed. Ed was a very good soul and a true friend. He always acted in his friends' best interest. He was to be the most reliable in the bunch of boys. Ed also unlike other adolescents, was comfortable in his own skin. His nickname was Troll. He somewhat resembled a fable character that crawled from under a bridge. Both of his friends spit oversized and soggy tobacco plugs from their mouths and rolled them up in plastic wrap, stuffing them in their pants pockets to be retrieved after church. In explanation, Dalton, one of Wally's pals, smiled, whispering, "Don't wanna waste the good stuff. Hey, Wally, want some Copenhagen for today's serpent show? I bet Ole Zerubbabel gets bit today and it will be by the copperhead. Or better yet, Emi-May, the choir director, gets bit on the ass by the asp!" The boys chuckled in unison.

"Naw!" Ed said, shaking his head. "I hope it's that nasty six-foot timber rattler that gits Deacon Connard. He deserves it. He's always givin' me the evil eye when I grab the mints in the vestibule. Heck, they're there fer us, ain't they? Thet old man should eat three 'cause his breath stinks like cow manure, an' he smells like whiskey and tobacco, all in one. Durned old hypocrite!" Ed added as he put his hands on his hips.

Wally flattened his lips and gently shook his head. "Handlin' deadly snakes?" Wally quoted with adolescent authority: *"An' Jesus answered him, "It is also written: Do not put the LORD your God to the test.""*

Mike, another chum smiled as he joined the group, "Wally, you really musta done paid attention in Sunday School! Okay, I got my dip and I'm ready fer the serpent show." Mike added, "an' I'm sitting in the back, just in case. I ain't getting bit! An' my mamma won't see me dippin," Wally smirked, with some borrowed chewing tobacco already showing between his front teeth.

The boys slid into the very back pew, positioning themselves towards the middle aisle, which provided them clear views of Stacy, Angela, and Kelly. Angela did a quick head turn to make eye contact with Mike, who returned her glance with a smile, raising his eyebrows in his best Tom Selleck imitation. Shelly blushed slightly and suppressed a giggle. Ed turned to Mike and snickered with his fist over his mouth and whispered, "ya dog!"

Mike innocently responded, "What?"

Just then, the service began with the routine greeting from the rural preacher. "Good mornin', brethrin. Welcome to another blessed day of warshep. PRAISE GOD! Let's get ready to warshep!" Pastor Zerubbabel announced, imitating boxing announcer Michael Buffer, *"Are ya ready to rumble?"* Instantly few murmurs of acknowledgement came from the congregation in support of Pastor Z's request. "We are the true followers. Let's begin our service to the LORRRD Jesus. Sista-B., please lead us in song and warshep.

Sister Betterthenue, the designated praise and worship leader, raised her plump hands, palms to the ceiling, and warbled, "Come on, church, time to praise the Lord! Make a noise before the Almighty. We are the warriors for the Lord. There is a great battle wagin' against the clutches of Lucifer. Ohh, Lord, fella believers, we must fight and stand strong in the Lord. The Prince of Lies, wants our souls! The Devil wants our children's souls. But the Devil has no chains to use on the holy ones. We are the holy ones. Let us sing the Lord's praises!" she finished as trumpet sounds blasted through the dusty speakers that released a distorted static sound that echoed throughout the building.

"Amen Sista," Pastor Z reinforced her declaration of spiritual warfare.

"Congregation, let's begin responsive worship!! Added Sista-B., who started the congregation's response by directing the church members, "God's People, say we're ready to fight." The voices of the congregation responded, yelling "We are ready to fight the wicked one!". Whatcha gonna do?" Sista-B responded, cupping her hand behind her right ear.

"STEP ON THE DEVIL'S HEAD!" came the response with simultaneous foot stomps on the old wooden floor. Sista-B called, "Ever'body, say we are ready to fight!"

The congregation responded, "We're ready to fight!" Sista-B asked, "Ever'body, whacha gonna do!?"

"STEP ON THE DEVIL'S HEAD!"

"Whacha gonna do?!

"Louder!"

"STEP ON THE DEVIL'S HEAD!."

"Agin?!"

"STEP ON THE DEVIL'S HEAD!!"

The fat congregational cheerleader kept up a beat, clapping her hands. Each time the small congregation responded, they stomped their feet. The old wooden floor in the small sanctuary felt as if it was going to drop to the basement below. Finally, as Sista-B lowered her hands, the small group became silent.

At that point, the pastor leaped across the stage, shouting, "PRAISE THE LORD! LORD GOD WILL BE VICTORIOUS OF ALL THE EARTHLY EVIL!. Eve ate the fruit. The female caused the curse. Humans have been thrown from the Garden, never to re-enter until the Lord returns. My fella believers, prepare! The Rapture is coming! We will be transported to Heaven at the second Coming of Christ. He will gather His followers and take them to Heaven. Forever in the Lord's presence, we will walk on streets of gold. My brothers and sistas, let us leave the heathens behind and prove that truly, we are God's people!"

Just then, a deacon named Michael, who stood in the back, two pews from the boys, began muttering in an unfamiliar language, as heads turned in the small church; people anticipated the elderly man's change in deportment. He dropped his cane and hopped around in a circle, then moved towards the front of the church. He seemed to be in a trance as more strange words uttered from his mouth. No one knew what he was saying, but then a woman called Sista Maybell began to interpret the unfamiliar language. Dalton looked at Mike and rolled his eyes, while Wally closed his eyes and then stared at the floor at his feet. "Here we go…here comes the gibberish," he whispered, shaking his head in disbelief as a small droplet of tobacco juice leaked down from his lower lip and splattered on the floor. Ed, noticing, snickered. Meanwhile, Deacon Michael's voice rose in volume.

"OOOObala, OObabla Doctrina est, quod vastum solidum, tollet mala super terram, Sarracenis erit tantum religio, ego autem vadam ad balneo, Christus est primum redire, im vereor ne non exspiravit, tollet serperpt in orbe terrarum, OOObala, Oobabla!"

Zerubbabel strode to the center stage, standing in front of the pulpit. He began to translate. "God speaks to us! God says. The Lord will have mercy on his flock. Not one sheep will be left behind. The Christian doctrine is the true and only word of God. Prepare! Jesus is coming soon! A worldwide event is coming to separate the wheat from the chaff. The weeds will burn and we shall be snatched up with Jesus. We will meet our Lord in the sky. We must prove to the Lord our complete devotion. We must control the devil's influence. It's time to control the serpent! God says, God says!"

As the pastor shouted, Wally, whose face suddenly had taken on a greenish tint, looked at his friends and mumbled, I feel sorta dizzy."

Mike, with eyebrows raised, and whispered. "Ya dumb dupe, did y'all swoller the juice?!"

Mouth suddenly dry, Wally nodded. "Aah, I'm gonna throw up!" he gasped, and cupping his hands over his mouth,. He jumped up and bolted for the bathroom. He blasted through the sanctuary doors and entered the small lavatory, pushing open the single stall's door with his right hand. Observing this commotion, the Deacon Downer, the usher near the back pew, shouted in a judgmental tone, "Boy ya sick? You juveniles been drinkin' and partyin' again. You're all young heathens, doin' the Devil's work!"

In response, Mike muttered, "Aah, shut up. ya old pretentious hypocrite!"

Meanwhile, Wally, leaning over the toilet bowl, had a gut wrench and spewed vomit into the toilet. Two more deep heaves produced green bile pouring out his mouth with small flakes of Copenhagen scattered in the vile vomit. Still dizzy and mouthwatering, he could feel the burning from the acidic gastric juices in his throat. Rinsing his mouth and wiping his face with some brown paper towels from the dispenser on the wall, Wally made his way back to his pew beside his friends, purposely avoiding eye contact with everyone staring at him. Ed covered his mouth with his clenched fist and snickered. Although, trying not to make a sound his shoulders wore quivering.

As his stomach aching from the retching, Wally sat in agony, waiting for the service to end. As he looked around the room that was still whirling, it appeared to him that the sanctuary's spinning was speeding up. All he could do was to close his eyes and rest his face in his hands. Trying desperately to make it stop. Dalton, with an attempt at some sympathy, whispered, "I told you not to swaller.!" All Wally could think was, *"Is he stupid? Does he think I didn't hear him? Aah, when is this going to end?"*

CHAPTER 2
JESUS LOVES YOU

Many members were fanning themselves with their service programs, inside the sanctuary temperature over ninety degrees that morning.

Looking to the rear of the church, Pastor Dr. Bruce said, "Usher Jacob, could you please lower the temperature? These good sheep like it at seventy-two degrees to worship our Good Shepherd. Thank you." Turning to the congregation, Pastor Bruce continued, "Good morning, church family, welcome to our house of worship." She said to those attending the contemporary 8:30 AM service. "If this is your first time visiting Good Shepherd Community Church," we offer you a special welcome!!" A rush of cool air began to fall from the ceiling vents, as one by one, the waving programs disappeared. "Maybe this cool air will make this fiery sermon a little more tolerable." The racially diverse loving congregation chuckled in unison, aware that Pastor Bruce was a passionate black women and only preached peace and forgiveness. Never the Bible thumper and accusatory type. She based all messages on strengthening relationships with God, friend or foe. Her messages echoed, "What would Jesus NOT do." And that was turned people away.

"Today, we're going to worship the Lord in a very very special way! We pray that we open our hearts to others. Let's also be openminded to those with differing opinions and with understanding. Let us reach out to others, even though disagreement. Fill us with agape love! Love God, love people, love life, love each other. Rachel, please lead us in song."

The young attractive Latino guitarist in the small musical ensemble started with a short run down the neck of her vintage Martin acoustic and then began the melody of "I Can Only Imagine." The Jamaican drummer struck his crash cymbal and then maintained a perfect base rhythm for the multi-cultural congregation to sing. Rachel waved her right hand above her shoulder, beckoning the nearly eight hundred parishioners to join in song.

When the song was finished, Pastor Bruce stepped to the pulpit, closed her eyes and began to pray aloud. "Dear Lord, use me today to relay a worthy message to your sheep." Opening her eyes and looking down at her congregation, she announced, "This sermon has been heavy on my heart all week. It's a sermon that God has placed in my heart and I pray this message speaks to your hearts," she added with a serious stare but also with a warm, gentle and sincere smile.

"Today's message is about a little man who many think is just a short and cute, little, round, fat guy. Ya know, kinda like a Biblical Fred Flintstone. But unknown to many, there's an evil associated with this character. Some of us don't understand the society of Roman rule." At that moment, out onto the stage, a little short guy walked on his knees. His costume appeared as if it was directly out of a child's picture Bible. This little fellow wore oversized sandals attached to his knees that made a flip-flop sound as he crossed the wooden floor of the stage. Then he climbed up a prop sycamore tree and waved to the congregation. He was very animated, causing laughter throughout the worship center. As if on cue, children moved from the front pew to the steps leading up to the stage. One little guy named Jared, in his Virginia Cavalier bow tie, reached up and grabbed the mike attached to the pulpit and said "Hi Mommy!!" The congregation laughed again, as warm smiles filled the sanctuary. In unison, all the children cried. "Zacchaeus, come down from that sycamore tree!" Their little voices began singing.

Zacchaeus was a wee little man
And a wee little man was he
He climbed up in a sycamore tree
For the Lord he wanted to see

And when the Savior passed that way
He looked up in the tree
And said, 'Zacchaeus, you come down!
For I'm going to your house today!
For I'm going to your house today!'

Zacchaeus was a wee little man
But a happy man was he
For he had seen the Lord that day
And a happy man was he;
And a very happy man was he

The congregation clapped for a long minute. Pastor Bruce stepped from behind the stage curtain as the children exited, filing out of the service center to the youth center in the basement of the church. Pastor Bruce smiled and addressed her congregation, asking, "Doesn't it always warm your heart to hear from God's children?" Then she began her message.

"Folks, we love how that song depicts Zacchaeus, the tax collector. The little actor, remaining in the simulated sycamore tree, waved to the crowd; Pastor Bruce chuckled and then continued, "This song doesn't represent the truth about the time period. Tax collectors were representatives of Roman control. You see, tax collection in Roman times was not pleasant. Well, we all know that paying taxes is never pleasant, (A few laughs could be heard.) Most of us dread filing out the tax forms and gathering financial records…but we complete the forms and mail them in. The citizens of Jericho knew that Zacchaeus was the tax controller. He was a *tax farmer,* a term used during this period. The common people of Jericho also knew that Zacchaeus charged more money than needed and kept extra for himself. People were afraid to complain because the Roman Empire and its soldiers were feared, Zacchaeus was the informant, "tattle tell" if you will. As the Bible says many times in the words of God, tax collectors were the same as thieves. Tax collectors were despised, known as traitors that worked for the Romans and not the Jewish community."

"Now as this story in Luke 19:1-10 reveals, let's consider Christ's popularity. Word of His miracles and teachings had spread across the Holy land. The common people viewed Jesus as a high priest. It was customary for the people to greet high-ranking officials before entering the city. Following this tradition, a large group ventured beyond the walls of Jericho to greet Jesus on his journey to Jerusalem and the road passed through Jericho. Today, we would call this a parade; the citizens lined the streets. Many townspeople escorted Him through the gate; many invited Jesus to have dinner at their home. Jesus declined, explaining that he was just passing through to Jerusalem. While Jesus was passing through the gate to Jericho, a blind man, Bartimaeus, called out to Jesus. 'Son of David, have mercy on me' and left his cloak. He gave up his only possession to be with Jesus. The townspeople tried to hush the beggar. Nevertheless, Jesus knew Bartimaeus's heart and gave sight back to the man. The miraculous healing gave the lowest citizen new life and self-worth. The religious townspeople did not understand the magnitude of Christ influence by this miraculous act of kindness to this blind beggar."

"But again the Pharisees invited Jesus to the synagogue to see the temple. 'Come look and see what we have prepared for you, rabbi.' Jesus responded, 'Thank you, but I'm on my way to Jerusalem.' As Jesus walked through Jericho, Jesus looked up into the sycamore tree; hidden in the branches was the little man, afraid. With a stern command, Jesus said, 'Zacchaeus, come down from that tree.'"

"Reluctantly, Zacchaeus came down from his safe haven, although frightened but curiously intrigued, Zacchaeus, with shuffling short steps, made his way to Jesus. Christ looked deep into the eyes of the short little man and said, 'Today I will eat at your house.'"

"Disappointed, confused and angered, comments rose throughout the crowd, especially among the Pharisees. 'Why does the rabbi give acknowledgement to a sinner and a beggar? We teach God's laws and care for the synagogue!'"

The pastor continued. "Christ knew their hearts, that they had great faith and believed that through Him each would receive salvation. Christ knew their souls. Christ saw the sincerity in both men; desire to have a relationship with God. The hearts of Zacchaeus and Bartimaeus hearts were both sincere. Zacchaeus was the wealthiest man in the city, this tax farmer had everything the world had to offer. Zacchaeus was empty inside and wanted something more. With all his heart, he believed that the wonders and teachings of Jesus would fill this void. He believed that the only way is through Jesus. Bartimaeus, begging for scraps, had the least in the town. His only procession was a cloak and he left it to be with Jesus."

Pausing, Pastor Bruce addressed the congregation. "My sheep, we must understand the significance of the two believers in this story. As each God-loving man walked across the planet in this Biblical time, these individuals were looking for a better life. Jesus personally gave these men a worthy and meaningful life. Bartimaeus was given sight. He was freely given a means to care for himself, which in turn provided evidence of God walking amongst his people. Zacchaeus, seeking a better way, quite possibly a means to relieve and forgive himself for overwhelming guilt, allowed Jesus to become the center of his life."

"Even so, the religious leaders found it confusing that these two sinners had gained Christ's attention while they had been ignored. Now listen to this: Jesus isn't concerned about what we can build on this earth, not material things we can acquire or the status we can achieve in our community. He wants us to develop strong relationships so that we build others up so that we can spend eternal life with God Almighty."

"So you see, my brothers and sisters, it doesn't matter to Jesus how many sins you have accumulated in your life or the size of your bank account. He wants you fully for Himself and to shower you with love. Love unimaginable! Just as the daylight surrounds your bodies, He wants to surround your being! Amen. Thank you Lord Jesus. Let's move closer to Him every day, my brethren." The pastor paused for a moment to allow her message to sink in. "In closing, let's be assured that Jesus wants to be in your heart no matter your financial influence or the deepest poverty, church Jesus wants to have a personal relationship with you. The son of the creator of the Universe wants to be your personal strength."

Turning to the small group to the side, she said, "Rachel, would you again lead us in song? As we sing "Jesus Is Calling," please close your eyes, and if you felt the Holy Spirit call you today, come down front so we can pray for you. The decision is yours and Jesus is calling you. Come acknowledge your desire to have a personal relationship with Him."

After many of the congregation had filed to the front of the church to shake the pastor's hand and receive her blessing, she announced, "Now church, if you have a committed relationship with our Lord, I invite you to take communion with us. Ushers, please distribute the cups."

As the ushers passed each row of pews, Pastor Bruce added, "And when he had given thanks, he broke it, and said, 'Take, eat: this is my body, which is broken for you: this do in remembrance of me. After the same manner, also he took the cup, when he had supped, saying; this cup is the New Testament in my blood: this do, as often as ye drink it, in remembrance of me.'

"Brother and sisters, we have provided a special treat for the first day of April. We have a large meal in the basement of the church. Our local Chinese members of the *Flaming Wok Restaurant* chain have provided a meal in the community center downstairs. God bless you and hope that you join us for food and fellowship...."

CHAPTER 3
REPTILE REVIVAL

Wally looked around the sanctuary still whirled. Rubbed his stomach and mouth dry as he tried to swallow the acidic stomach juices that remained in his throat. As he sat in agony, Dalton said, "Here we go! Holy revival via serpentine survival." Sista-B lifted her arms with hands fluttering. She looked like someone warming up for athletic event. She repeated the same body movements every Sunday. Dalton repeated his earlier comment, eyebrows drawn down, "I hope she gets bit on the ass by the asp." Dalton had seen the routine many times and the predictability of the ritual irritated him. Dalton shook his head with skepticism, repeated under his breath, "revival via serpentine survival."

Brother Paul joined Sista-B in his predictable routine he clapped his hands and began jumping up and down. His fat belly jiggled and his starched white shirt became untucked. Brother Paul's white hairy belly became visible. His belly lapped over his black leather belt and as he bounced the fat roll, mass lifted up revealed the large silver Harley Davidson Emblem.

Ed said with a snicker, "Look at that lard ass!" Making eye contact with Mike, "if I become that guy, just shoot me!" He made a nimble fist and continued to snicker as his head slightly tossed back. Repeated "look at that lard ass…"

Wally shook his head, eyebrows pressed, "But I don't want her to die. Sista-B is just doing what the egomaniac preacher thinks is godly spiritual worship. Seriously! It's nothing but brainwashin, simple as that! God loves us and we show love back by loving and caring for others," his headshake continued with a deep serious concerned stared into his friends eyes.

The faithful followers on the stage beheld the venomous snakes, as cages were rolled out one by one. Sista-B was first, she grabbed the asp. Paul, the lead deacon, picked up the largest snake, a seven-foot timber rattler, and wrapped it around his neck. Every time it rattled its tail, he would spin in circles. He loved the snake so much, after Wednesday night choir practice, Brother Paul would give it an extra rat. He considered it his pet. Pastor Zeb grabbed one of the copperheads; memorized by the markings on its back, beautifully reddish-brown cross bands shaped like an hourglass. He stroked the belly of the native snake. Farmer Brown donated it to the church; he collected from the nearby hay fields.

Deacon Connard picked up the last specimen. Barney, as most folks called him, wore a flowery bow tie. Some say he resembled Deputy Barney Fife of the Andy Griffith Show. As he handled the docile snake his hair would fall in his face and his eyes were wide and round. His mannerisms resembled Barney, saying, "nip it, nip it in the bud." He grabbed the prized Mamba. He took pride in the selection of the biggest most feared snake. He would parade it up and down the aisle, as if he would gain more manly respect. The wise old-time parishioners knew his facade and giggled as he passed by their pew.

The ceremonial trance dance started. The drummer struck his Tom toms. The beat sounded an Indian warpath rhythm. The faithful follower's eyelids fluttered. Their eyes rolled upward and each disciples' whites of their eyes became visible to the on looking congregation.

Ed looked at his pals, "this ain't nothing but a freakin circus. The same worshippers doing the same behaviors every week what a bunch of freaks." More phrases that seemed replicating Hebrew language resonated throughout the small sanctuary.

Eyes wide open in disbelief, whispered Dalton, "Old Pastor Zeb has a cult. I cannot believe this foolishness. Tempting fate! Someone is going to die or catch a disease from this craziness. And it ain't gonna be me. I gotta get out of here!"

Sista-B stumbled on the pulpit step. Nearly fell on her knees and tried to catch her balance; she dropped the asp. The large dark snake slithered slowly into a defensive coil and the snake's ribbon body was in strike mode. Assessing its surroundings, the beast slithered its forked tongue back and forth. Asp's vertically pupil eyes were square on SistaB. Ms Betterthenue now out of the trance spun and tried to escape to the safety of the pulpit. As she turned the asp struck sinking the extended fangs into her buttocks. Screaming she tried to pull the serpent from under her skirt. The snake would not release its grip. To Sista-B it must have seemed like an eternity, but within seconds, it released the death grip, then Egyptian Cobra slithered down the pulpit step and hid under the front pew. All the church attendees jumped on top of the pews and ran for the nearest door. To Wally's surprise, Grandma Elder, sprang with her dress pulled to her knees. She leaped to the second pew's backrest and took long strides on each of the 15 pew backrests to the sanctuary exit and screamed "Lucifer is on the loose!"

Deacon Connard still held the Mamba, but now exhibited a facial fear that only Deputy Barney Fife could muster and express. In shock, he tried frantically to put the snake back into the cage. Before he could close the cage door, the snake in defense mode, precisely struck his man parts. The Mamba latched on and no matter what he did, it couldn't be pulled off his manhood. In a very loud squeal, he shouted, "Lord have mercy on me! Dear Lord the Jessabelle lured me into the adulterous relationship. Dear God let me live, and I will not cheat my employees ever again. Dear God do not let me die by this serpent. I want to be righteous in your eyes, please......"

Meanwhile, Sista-B in a fetal position bubbled foam from her lips. Zeb and the deacon were on the ground in agony. "Lord God relive this pain from the serpent's bite" Beckoned Pastor Zeb. But to no avail each man passed out under the severe pain. Toxic venom over took their bodies, and each became unconscious and death followed.

Dalton, Ed and Mike said simultaneously, "Let's get out of here!"

Dalton commanded, "git in my Toyota before we git snake bit. Pappa is waitin at the farm to take us to Rockingham to get on the Ashland Trolley Trail. Boys let's get the senior adventure started!! It's time to load up the horses."

CHAPTER 4
TURNER'S TRAGEDY

Kyle Gravitt dressed in his sport slacks and matching Nike Golf shirt, physically fit, handsome young man with a family at home that he loved dearly. The kind of devotion that would make other wives jealous. His coworkers looked up to him as he never missed an opportunity to say something positive to everyone he met. His plan was dressed and ready for his tee-time at the new public golf course. He planned to leave work at noon to play golf on this unseasonably warm spring day ahead. This was his first time at the new golf course. While in college, Kyle played golf; he missed his favorite sport. He worked over fifty hours a week at the Titulada Juice Factory in Tallahassee, Florida. He walked into his boss's office. Not focused on the workday ahead, *but he pictured swinging his oversized club and driving the ball directly down the middle of the green fairway number one. And then strolling to the golf cart which awaited a cold Heineken.* As he passed through the glass door of his boss's office, he saw his distraught director sitting at his shiny cherry executive desk.

"Did you hear?!" owner and CEO of the Titulada Juice Factory said in a soft, trembling voice. His boss adjusted his purple tie. Back and forth his boss used his thumb and index finger to adjust it for his comfort. Moving his tie, was a habit when he was under stress. He was a middle aged and spent more time chasing women than minding the forty year old business. Since high school, he was destined to take over the family business. Unlike the generation before him which focused on quality juice products, he was a Gen-X narrow minded selfish jerk. All he cared about was looking good.

Kyle the assistant was confused by the tone and the uncharacteristic nature of B.D. Titulada "Hear what sir?"

"Someone broke into Turner's home last night and shot him! It appears to be a breaking and entering that went bad. The kids escaped out their bedroom window. Turner's wife was wounded as she shielded the children exiting the first floor window. But thank God, it's not life threatening, and she will be released today from Randolph General Hospital." Kyle's boss showed some relief in his teary eyed and wrinkled face.

Kyle responded sympathetically, "Thank God for the kids' sakes. Losing one parent is bad, but thank God the children did not lose two!"

After a delay, Kyle regained his composure after the shocking news. "Did they take anything?"

"They opened his locked gun cabinet and took his 12 gauge Remington skeet shotgun and some cash. He fought the scoundrel off to give time for his wife and children to make an escape."

"Oh Jesus this is terrible; hope they catch the thief. I just spoke with Turner last night. He was told me that they had made plans to go Disney World next month. God! You just never know!"

"I hope they shoot the criminals before they get to jail." Titulada faked a sad face. "We lost a very good man here at work and in the community. Turner was one of our most faithful employees. We should shut down today, but we can't... We have to fill the communion order for the diocese of Atlanta. The shipment must be ready for pickup by tonight at five. "How we goin to keep production today?" Asked company president. In his mind, he had already thought that putting a lowed paid employee in Turner's place would look good to the board of directors. Mindfully calculating labor cost, the lower paid replacement would save one percent on balance sheet.

Kyle had a special way of working with people, and employees respected him. "Well, I will head to the production floor. I think our men and women will realize the urgency and get it done. Sir, they always do." Kyle was known for his team leadership and concern for others. He responded with a quick solution and offered confidence to his senior boss. "We have a new guy, John White. You know the guy sits by himself and never says more than three words to anybody. He deserves a chance he always fills in where I need him and he works independently with little supervision. We're lucky to have him: He is intelligent!"

"I think he shadowed Turner for about a week. We will have to ask him step up early. He should be able to handle the filling operation." Confidently stated Kyle.

"I hope so. Keep an eye on him today! We have to meet the quota. We cannot lose the diocese of Atlanta. The president responded with an anxious and precarious sound in his voice. Titulada thought to himself, *his company balance sheet would show a 1% increase in profits by losing Turner. I'll underpay his replacement.* In public, he had a charming smile, but his small group of managers knew it was just his narcissism-PR. They knew his true nature. He would sell out his mom to look good to the board of directors.

Kyle Gravitt met John White at the time clock, "Good morning and reached out his right hand."

White, confused by the morning greeting was taken by surprise that the morning shift supervisor approached him before the 8:00am team meeting. He made brief eye contact with his boss and said, "Uh yeah, mornin" with a mumble. He was trying to cover up his hang over from the night before. He turned and slid his vape pen into his cargo pants pocket. Turned back towards his shift supervisor and said, "Yes, is something I can do for you." He focused on Kyle's face and turned his ear slightly to block out the background machinery noise.

"We are in a desperate situation this morning and the company needs your help to keep production going! Many of us are hurting. Steve Turner was murdered last night in his home. The police believe it was a random home invasion. Steve tried to defend his home. He successfully protected his kids and wife. Some slayer killed him."

"Oh damn," White's demeanor changed. "Sir I'm sorry." John White did not have a surprised or alarmed facial expression. "Sir, I know he was liked by many and the other production floor employees relied on him. What can I do to help?"

Slightly puzzled by White's reaction to the tragic news, Kyle paused, *why did he not appear to be surprised* and then asked, "We need someone to cover and supervise the filling machine. Do you think you can handle this? I realize you have only been here three weeks." Kyle was somewhat desperate to overcome the loss of his dear friend, Steve Turner.

"Yes sir, I have been watching and listening to Mr. Turner. He is, uh, was." John White displayed compassion with a slight downward tilt with his chin trying to emulate the emotions the other employees were experiencing by the shocking news.

"Okay then, I appreciate it. I will be in the office if you need help. Pick up the info phone, and I will assist you." Kyle in an appreciative tone, "Again thanks for steppin up."

White turned his back and walked away confident that the first part of his mission was completed. He grabbed his Black Galaxy Fold phone and texted: "The WASP is in position to STING!"

CHAPTER 5
SADDLE UP BOOY'S

The four boys traveled north on Route 340 to the trailhead in Rockingham County. Mike looked out his window and saw the Blue Ridge Mountains.

"Wow, those are pretty hills!" he exclaimed.

"They ain't exactly hills," Dalton remarked.

"Well, they're still pretty!" Mike growled.

The midday sun was shining down on the bluish mountain landscape miles away. Pappa, with his stereo dialed into a Christian radio station, turned up the volume inside the 2017 Super Duty Ford-450 Lariat, what the boys called the "West Virginia Cadillac."

Dalton announced, "Y'all git ready, boys, Pappa's gonna sing!"

His announcement was met by a chorus of loud groans as Johnny Cash's version of "When the Man Comes Around" resonated through the Harmon 10 speaker sound system.

"Dalton's grandad began…"*There's a man goin around takin names and he decides who to free and who to blame"* Dalton interrupted Pappa, announcing, "This is our turn off, Pappa."

Wally looked at Google maps on his iPhone said, "Yep, he's right, this is it. Take a right here, onto Stoney Mountain Drive."

The truck bounced on the rough gravel road for five minutes as the horses, suddenly startled, kicked the doors of the six-horse trailer.

As the truck came to a stop, Big Red whinnied and kicked the stall door one more time to register his displeasure.

"You ready to git out, big boy?" Dalton called as he opened the door to the long horse trailer. Reaching in, he gave each horse an apple and then unloaded them --- the horses, not the apples. Ed took the reins and walked his horse over to hitching post. Wally and Mike led their horses over beside Ed's and tied them securely. Pappa directed the boys, showing them how to secure the camping gear on the saddles.

"Well, good luck, have fun, cowboys!" he chuckled as the stillagile old man slid back onto his seat, waved, and stuck his head back out the window, and shouted, "See y'all at Massanutten!"

As the boys waved and waited for the dust to settle, Dalton said, "Hope you all got your provisions, men. Saddle up, we gotta get goin'!"

It wasn't more than five minutes along the well-worn trail that he turned in his saddle and laughed.

"Did you see that dork Deacon Connard take that snake bite in the scrotum?" I think he confessed to every fornicated act since 7th grade. Wally smiled.

Ed snickered, rocked back and forth while holding onto the horn of this western saddle.

Dalton laughed aloud. "Served him right. He has used people all his wretched existence.

Dalton snarled and then started to gallop his red thoroughbred. "Come on boy, let's git it." The other horses followed, and the boys trotted up the rock covered trail.

"Hey, there's the sign for Indian Grave Ridge. We're camping there tonight! Says we're only half a mile out. We're already losin' daylight. The sun's gonna set soon. We gotta hurry up 'cuz we need some light to set up the hammocks." Dalton gave Big Red a kick and horse and rider started ahead at a full gallop. Wally gave his horse a slap with the reins to catch up and match Dalton's pace.

Mike grunted, "Oh no!" His boots were not fully in the stirrups and began to bounce off the saddle. He was out of syn. Without control, Ed's horse joined the others. Meanwhile, Ed, was hanging on for dear life.

Arriving at the camping area with darkness threatening. The boys dismounted and tied the horses up for the evening. The spot they had selected was in a clearing, surrounded by four large hemlocks. The low branches were easy to secure their hammocks to, in addition created a shelter to prevent the night's dew from collecting on the boys.

The space between the giant tree trunks was an ideal location for an evening fire, something previous campers had decided, evidenced by the circle of rocks, wood ash and a small pile of unused kindling. Mike searched the area for some dry wood and pine cones while the others unloaded the horses. A warm fire was soon crackling, the flames silhouetted against the surrounding darkness as the boys crawled into the parachute silk hammocks for the evening.

With the comfort of the fire burning, Wally stared up at the circle of night sky. The dim new moon made the night sky velvet black, a perfect night for stargazing. No clouds and no artificial light made the night an unbelievable sight. Never, had Wally seen so many stars and the clarity to pick out all the major constellations. He began to name each and added, "Modern astronomy uses two terms to identify a collection of stars: the term most commonly used is *constellations.* However, smaller groups are called *asturias* or *asterisms*" he added. "Pelaides and the Hyades are both *asterisms,* and each lies within the boundaries of the constellation Taurus. Another example is the northern asterism popularly known as the Big Dipper, composed of the seven brightest stars within the area of the defined constellation of Ursa Major. Most folks just think the Big Dipper is a constellation by itself cause it's easy to see, but it isn't."

In his hammock, Ed scratched his forehead and asked, "How d'ya know all this stuff?"

"Yeah," Mike added, "is there gonna be a test on Monday?!"

Meanwhile, Dalton, still enthralled by the astronomical spectacle above, just murmured, "Man is so small. We are totally insignificant in comparison to the vastness of the universe. Tonight's sky makes me understand what" Carl Sagan meant when he kept saying, *"billions and billions* of stars."

Mike added, "Bill Nye said *Woah.*"

"Yeah, I remember that Bill Nye, the Science Guy special on TV," Ed's voice added in the flickering darkness, "You know, and how did the universe form? That's the *big* question. I enjoyed my online astronomy class when the high school couldn't schedule one 'cause there were too many other science classes."

Mike added, "It was because none of the teachers were certified to teach astronomy!"

Returning to his lecture mode, Wally continued, "The current scientific dogma believes it was a totally random explosion, the Big Bang. A psalm of David says, *"The heavens declare the glory of God, and the sky above proclaims his handiwork."* Having been exposed to both explanations, I lean towards God's creation,"

"I trust in the Lord Almighty," Wally began as the others listened. "Just think about the distance the Earth is from the sun. It's perfect!! A twenty-three and one-half degree angle toward the sun. If slightly different the earth burns up or slightly the other direction, we freeze! Can't believe that's random."

"Yeah, well. So who lit the match?" scoffed Ed.

"Yeah, that's hard to argue with, considering the evidence available to mankind" responded Wally. "Ya know, there are so many things about the celestial realm that allow the sustainment of life on earth. The twenty-three and one-half degree on its axis is the perfect control of sunlight striking the earth for water to exist in three states of matter. If the angle should change to twenty-five during the summer, the North Pole water would nearly boil, and the southern hemisphere would freeze to forty-five degrees south latitude. It's darn miraculous. Without three states of matter, life would not exist," Wally concluded.

"Well, my personal theory about the Big Bang is that God was working on his Science Fair project an' stuck his finger in a cloud of hydrogen...and *bang!*" Mike inserted with a chuckle.

Dalton broke up the conversation as he stared into the yellow-blue flames of the campfire. "Geez Wally, do you ever think about normal stuff, like pretty girls and goin' fishing? Get some sleep, guys, we got a long ride tomorrow."

CHAPTER 6
THE BAD NEWS

"Good evening from Fox News, I'm George Michael, and this is your latest news tonight. Thousands are dead. Entire churches that were seen as sanctuaries now have people lying lifeless all over the Southeast, although no true cause has been determined. Many small children are alive, but nearly all adults are deceased. Our Fox News team is reporting this developing story: on the screen, you can see the individual team correspondents: Marianna MacNamee in rural Virginia, Sylvester Adams in Boone, North Carolina, and Evelyn Jefferson is located Atlanta, Georgia. Sylvester, what's the scene like in Boone?" anchor George Michael asked with a distraught expression on his handsome face.

There was a slight delay in Sylvester Adam's response. "Evening, George. I'm here, reporting from Good Shepard Church, a very large worship center here in Boone. Speaking with one of the ushers, he informed us that at least eight hundred people were in the congregation today. Of those attending, five hundred ninety-eight adults and adolescents have perished! Initial examination shows no trauma or physical injury to the bodies. It appears that all died instantly from some unknown agent. We have not been allowed to enter the church. We were told that one of the police officers in the basement of the church watched members of the congregation die. He said they just dropped after eating a catered lunch from a local Chinese restaurant chain. The entire facility has been declared a crime scene and has been roped off with police tape. We can see from the parking lot that a HAZMAT team has arrived, dressed in blue biohazard suits. In addition, three forensic epidemiologists are about to enter the building."

The camera switched back to the lead anchor, "Are there any reasons for the deaths? Does anyone have a guess or possible explanation for this massive mortality rate?"

Addressing the lead anchor's question, Sylvester Adams ran a hand across his shaved head as he shook it. "At this time, no solid, reliable explanation. We've learned that today was a regular church service and that after the service, not all -- but many -- members went to the basement for a brunch. Some early speculation points to the catered food being a source or the agent causing the deaths. No one knows, and it's too early for anyone to hypothesize."

"Thank you Sylvester. How about the situation in Atlanta, Evelyn?" The camera left George Michael and quickly shifted to a large white church. The sun sparkled on the top of the steeple and strangely, the camera angle produced a halo around the top of the gold cross. The view slowly moved from the church to focus on Evelyn Jefferson, a middle-aged, slightly overweight brunette, who briefly nodded and began her report.

"This church has lost 793 people, mostly adults and adolescents, but there are twenty-seven children under the age of ten also dead. Strangely, any children under four are alive, but it's unclear why age. We have not been allowed to enter the church. A HAZMAT team was already in the church when we arrived. Despite the number of deceased, it appears that forty-seven adults among the congregation are alive and are showing no symptoms or obvious distress. They are being isolated in the multi-purpose section of the church. The entire community here in Atlanta is in shock. In addition, we understand that nine other churches in the Atlanta area have reported that many of their people are dead."

"Thank you, Evelyn, our thoughts and prayers are with the Christian families of Atlanta. Our country is dealing with one of the most horrible events in American history. It appears that thousands are dead since this morning, with no one able, at this time, to determine the cause. The rising death toll is overwhelming, beyond disastrous. What do we see in Virginia?"

Pictured on the screen was Marianna MacNamee and in the background a small church resting at the base of a tree-covered mountain.

"At the Holiest Tabernacle, a relatively small church, of the fiftythree that arrived here this morning, forty-one are dead. The parishioners are lying dead, scattered both inside and outside this small church. The preliminary report here is similar to the deaths being reported at the bigger churches, with approximately 80% dead. Because the Virginia state police have the two roads blocked, our crew had to walk half a mile to get to the church. The county coroner is here, a few nurses, and a local doctor are also on the scene. This rural community is short on medical resources, so we don't have a lot to report at the moment. A volunteer paramedic is here with us, and he informed us that the congregation is known to be members of a snake-handling church. In addition, he reported that two HAZMAT teams are in route from Richmond and Charlottesville. I have one eyewitness. Malachi, did you see what happened?" the relatively young blond reporter asked, turning to a man who appeared to be in his early forties.

"Yeah, Ah did. The'm snakes got loose, killed'm all!" the man said excitedly with a somewhat moronic half-grin on his thin face.

Marianna MacNamee looked, shocked, her eyes wide open. Obviously, she had not been expecting either his answer or the country accent...or both still, she kept her composure while one could guess that some viewers across the nation laughed. "Did you say snakes killed your church members?" asked the recovered MacNamee.

"Yeah, ma'm. Sister Betty was first to let her snake go. Before it was over, all them snakes was loose and folks was gittin' bit. Mah wife is dead! Can't find mah son, don' know where he's at!"

Just then, another man passed by Malachi, who, ignoring the camera, abruptly asked, "Have you seen Wally?" The fellow church attendee, tears in his eyes, did not respond, and appeared to be in shock with a zombie's blank face as he staggered away. Malachi turned back to look at Marianna MacNamee, who asked another question.

"Did all the members get bitten by snakes?"

"Uhh, don' know, but most are dead. Gotta be the snakes. Ya know they're evil. Demons on Earth. Yeah, they're evil! Killed my wife, killed all mah friends!" The man called Malachi began to sob.

The camera shifted back to George Michael, who was nearly tearing up. "The church-going citizens of the United States appear to be under attack by an invisible enemy…or enemies! We will be on the air continuously to keep you informed." Trying to fight his distressed emotional state, he continued, "Up next, Kevin Rawson with the latest up-to-the-minute, Super-Radar weather." The usually composed news anchor rubbed his forehead and slowly wiped the tears from his eyes as the picture faded and the station's logo filled the screen.

CHAPTER 7
POISON SUMAC?

After the first night, the boys woke up to the sounds and aroma of Dalton preparing breakfast. The sizzle of fresh trout in the black, castiron pan, seasoned by many fishing overnights, along with the rush of the clear mountain stream nearby made the temporary camp tranquil and peaceful. The equally seasoned and confident country boy had used his seven-foot-long fly rod before dawn to catch four, foot-long endemic brook trout in the vibrant Virginia stream.

"Man, something smells good!" Wally grunted as he rubbed his eyes after a peaceful night's sleep in the crisp Appalachian air.

Ed slid out of his sleeping bag and reached out for his boots. "Yeah, it does! Whaterya cookin'?"

"Brook trout," Dalton, still in his hip waders, replied as he flipped the fish that spattered melted butter onto the top of his hand. Dalton waved his hand in the air to soothe the burn. "Ouch! that's gonna blister."

"Where did *they* come from?" Ed wanted to know as he rubbed the sleep from his eyes.

"Have ya noticed that stream we're camped next to?" Dalton muttered somewhat sarcastically. "Ya know, this here country boy can survive, my friend. Ya know the song."

"Yep Hank William junior, *skin a buck and run a trotline*" responded Ed.

"YEAH that's right, used my elk-hair caddis and spotted ambush points behind those big boulders. The trout hide in eddies at the base of them and wait for the prey carried by the riffle. All ya gotta do is throw your floating line above the boulder and wait for the twitch."

Wally and Ed looked at each other, the latter saying, "I'm sure glad he's out here with us. I'm hungry. I could eat a horse…or a fish." Wally with terribly tousled bed head hair billowed in the breeze as he nodded in agreement.

Just then, Mike emerged from the woods said, "Man that was one humongous dump! I feel better," he announced as he finished zipping up his Wranglers as he neared the others. "Yeah, I had to go bad!"

"Gross!" Ed commented, adding, "and go wash your hands. What did you wipe with?"

"I was in a hurry and forgot my wipes. Used some leaves."

Dalton shook his head, "probably poison sumac.'

"Did it have three leaves? Glossy and hairy roots clinging to the tree?" Wally probed.

"No, they were just big ones on the ground, I don't know! I's in a hurry," Mike replied with a squeaky voice, "What's for breakfast?"

Each unpacked their mess kits from the saddlebags on their horses, which were totally uninterested in what Mike wiped his ass with (the horses, not the saddlebags). Dalton dished out equal portions of the trout, which slid smoothly into the aluminum dishes. Starved, the boys used their fingers and finished the fish in minutes. Mike said, "Durn them trouts went faster than brownies at a *Grateful Dead Concert.*"

Wiping the last bit of grease off his lips with the back of a sleeve, Mike looked at the horses staked in the meadow. "Aaah, that horse you gave me, Ed, ain't there! It musta untied itself, and I have no idea where it is. Durn you, Ed! I knowed you gave me that old mare for a reason."

Ed snickered, "You just gotta know how to talk to old Queen Silver."

Mike angrily snorted through his nostrils, which flared as his lips flattened. "Why'd ya ever name a *white horse Silver,* anyways?

"Mike, it's *knew*, not knowd. You sound so dumb when you talk like that. Ain't no such word as *knowed*" Also, ain't no word *anyways*, neither," said Ed, shaking his head.

Dalton commanded, "Just get Silver and get a saddle on her. Saddle em' up, Wally and you, too, Ed. An' it might rain this morning, so have your ponchos handy. We gotta make seventeen miles today to stay on our schedule. We'll camp at Zion Mountain; it's remote and we should have it all to ourselves. It has a shelter and a fishin' hole. If we catch a few, we can conserve our other food when we can't catch fish." It was Dalton's job to plan each day and night. The boys knew each camping spot had provisions, drinkable water, shelter, and potential trout dinners. "We can't get off schedule 'cause our supplies won't last!."

"Ed, where's that dagburn old nag?" Cried Mike, looking around frantically.

Ed snickered, placed his fingers under his tongue, pushed it back to the roof of his mouth and blew an ear-piercing whistle. The sound echoed off the steep rock cliff towering over the stream. Quickly, Queen galloped in and nuzzled Ed for an expected dried-apple reward. Her big yellow teeth showed as she curled up her lip and her tongue lifted the treat from his palm. "There you go, Mike, now she's ready for you, our equestrian Einstein," Ed said with a sarcastic snicker.

The trail was rocky. Granite boulders jutted out into the path and the horses had to move their wide bodies off the trail to negotiate the narrow path to avoid losing their footing, causing the boys to balance themselves in the stirrups. On one part of their journey, the trail ran along the edge of a cliff as the boys nervously looked down a twohundred-foot drop. If they took a quick look beyond the cliff, they found the view amazing. They could see a good thirty-five miles into the Shenandoah Valley from that outlook. The geology of the past was apparent; they could see how ice-age glaciers had plowed through the landscape, creating smooth mountains and valleys. Glacial till deposits scattered the mountains. Each boulder pile was left as the glaciers retreated thousands of years ago.

An hour later, after passing safely beyond the narrow path, Ed said, "That made my tailbone smoke a cigarette!"

"What the heck does *that* mean, ya countra bumpkin?"Mike asked, rolling his eyes.

"My dad always says that in a dangerous situation, you know, from fear, I guess."

"Yeah, I know whacha mean. That was scary lookin over those cliffs!" Mike added, letting out a long breath.

"Let's take a break. The horses need water and we can turn them out to graze in that meadow down there," Dalton suggested, pointing.

Jumping off his horse, Big Red, Ed snickered and with his fist near his lips, asked "How's yer ass, Mike?" Wally giggled.

After making some peanut butter wraps and honey, they munched on honey crisp apples. Mike kept half of his and put in his pocket. He did his best whistle, and Silver trotted towards him as Mike reached out his palm with the apple core. The old white mare curled her lip, stuck out her tongue, and lifted the core from his palm. "Thatta girl!" Mike rubbed her head and looked into Silver's glossy, bluish-gray eyes, which seemed to predict the beginning of a trusted relationship. Indeed, Mike realized he had a new friend. He realized there is more to a horse than just a huge, intimidating body. He then glanced at Ed.

Ed smiled. "Now you're getting to her! You got a friend forever."

Meanwhile, Dalton commanded, "Saddle up. Cowboys, time to make like horse crap."

"An' hit the trail." Wally finished.

CHAPTER 8
"WHEN THE MAN COMES AROUND."

Turning left off Clayton Drive, Dr. Tristan Snider listened to a street musician playing Johnny Cash's, *When the Man Comes Around.* As he waited at the long red light, top down on his 40 series 1974 Toyota Land Cruiser, he fixated on the verse sung by the vagabond:

"When the man comes around, the hairs on your arm will stand up, at the terror in each sip and in each sup, Will you partake of that last offered cup? Or disappear into the potter's ground.

As the green light flashed, Snider made eye contact with the street musician; he nodded his head to the man with the beat up old guitar. He shifted into first, released his clutch and sped off to his laboratory where his two colleagues awaited him. Dr. Snider entered the security gate and flashed his security badge. The world-renowned epidemiologist pulled into his designated parking space. Dr. Snider jumped down from his vintage SUV. His pace slow but direct to his lab at the *Center for Disease Control and Prevention* facility located on the CDC's *Edward R. Roybal Campus* in Atlanta, Georgia, the world's best at fighting the most infectious pathogens. Dr. Snider operated a sophisticated Biosafety Level-4 (BSL-4) facility. He and his team's BSL-4 unit is the highestcontainment laboratory in existence.

Dr. Snider bent his six foot four frame to the retinal scanner and the access alarm sounded. He had programed everything in his lab and the alarm was no exception. Vincent Price's voice sounded to grant entry. "Do you dare to enter the chamber," followed by Price's renowned Halloween laugh. As the first door opened, the outside air rushed into the small glass entry space. The entry door closed and sealed. He began to undress and started the thirty-minute routine to put on the blue bio-4 suit. First stage was the eight-minute chemical shower. Stepping into the next safety space, he then checked his suit for holes or other damages before putting it on. As he connected the many hoses, the air began to rush over his face. The airflow was loud and prevented from him hearing sounds in the sealed room.

He yelled, "Good morning Sunshine!" as Dr. Snider greeted his colleague.

Oh, he paused grinned and stated, should I address you as Dr. Withers." It was her first day back from her South Pacific honeymoon.

"I like the sound of Mrs. Withers," as she gave a little sigh with sparkles in her eyes and her face expressed a very satisfied smirk.

"Uhmmm, I believe I see fireworks in those blues eyes. Wow! That must have been some honeymoon!" Dr. Snider gave a wink to his lead researcher. It was difficult to see one another's face through the large protective mask. Each were yelling through the restrictive safety shield. Communication hindered by the sound of air in the sealed bio-4 blue suit.

Dr. Siribandu joined the conversation and directed it to a more serious tone, "Have you heard about the deaths in the Southeast?"

"Yeah, I expect a call soon from the brass," nodded Dr. Snider.

Dr. Withers spoke with anxiety and made eye contact with her teammates. She turned to both colleagues standing on the other side of the lab. She shouted, "It sure sounds suspicious. All the victims are associated with churches. From what I have been following, all the people were dead by Monday morning. Nobody reached a hospital alive. Scary the death toll is over eight thousand."

The three epidemiologists began their fifteen-minute break, mandatory because of the expended energy needed to maneuver in their awkward, blue bio-suits. The team started to exit the secure lab facility, the first step of the multi-step procedure being for each to shed the outer layer and hang it in their personal lockers. No mistakes could be tolerated, so each virologist needed to follow the strict exiting protocol, and also had to be highly alert as they exited the airtight room, for the exchange of air was the greatest risk of releasing a toxin into the natural world outside. The sliding doors hissed closed and after hearing the airlock- confirmation bell, the team moved to the small glassed room, which had a clear view of the bio-4 laboratory.

"It feels good to get this helmet off. It's hot and noisy in this thing. After two years, you'd think I'd be used to it," Dr. Withers said as she inhaled deeply, filling her chest with the cool filtered and sterile air of the break room and sat at the edge of the rectangular table.

"Yes, I agree. It always causes streaks in my makeup," Dr. Siribundo nodded her head and joined her colleague. She slumped into a plastic chair and sat at the opposite end of the table, facing her partner.

"Simple: don't wear makeup!" Dr. Snider chuckled as he reached into the refrigerator and grabbed a Gatorade; he sat down and began discussing the previous night's news. "Did you see FOX news last night and this morning?' he asked no one in particular with a baffled look on his face. "The evangelicals are still claiming it to be *THE* Rapture. Whole congregations are joining and praying. Nobody has ever seen religious gatherings like these, camping out on mountaintops, waiting for Christ!" Siribundo leaned towards the others, and whispered, "What are they calling the Rapture? For that matter, what is the Rapture?" Dr. Siribundo made quote signs with her index and middle fingers. She was puzzled for she raised Islamic.

"Well, many people have lived a full life waiting for the second coming of Christ. Good souls who have many times made our world a better place." Dr. Snider shook his head with a slight roll of the eyes. "Really, who knows? It could be happening. I am not one to judge. All I have control over is finding the reason why these people are dying Rapture, Really?"

A message appeared on the information screen in the bio-4 level lab. The team looked at the screen and glanced at each other. Dr. Snider said there it is. Garret Kincaid, M.D., NIAID Director appeared on the screen.

"We need answers! The President called this morning and wants an explanation. Rumors are flooding social media." The public fears the worse. Total death. Looting all across the US. We must have answers. The only good news is no one has died since Monday. Whatever the infective agent is; it must have originated at the churches. That is the common clue. But there is no guarantee that is where the outbreak will die." Our fear is the first responders have been infected and it is just time before it spreads throughout the south. We do not know what the next twenty four hours will bring!"

Dr. Snider responded yes sir, we're on it!

CHAPTER 9
WE NEED ANSWERS

"The idea of a Rapture rescue by Jesus sounds wonderful," said Leoni Siribondu with a smile.

Tristan smiled and boasted, "The second coming is soon. In fact, *Jesus promised His disciples that He would come again. John 14:1-3 says, "Let not your heart be troubled...In My Father's house are many mansions; if it were not so, I would have told you. I go to prepare a place for you. And if I go and prepare a place for you, I will come again and receive you to myself; that where I am, there you may be also."*

Withers shook her head, "Really? We must find the truth! There must be a logical explanation for these deaths, a *scientific or biological* reason for them, not something mystical. The nuts among the public can think this is some kind of religious event but…. All I have control over is finding the reason why these people have died! We need to collect information and find ground zero for the scourge. All fatalities seem to be related to just a few churches."

"Yes," Withers added to Tristan Sniders's observation. "But what's strange is that the churches are hundreds of miles apart. The proximity of each congregation to another can't be a factor...or so it seems. What could possibly connect one sector of a population to another, miles away?"

Siribundo, a usually quick thinker and excellent problem-solver, began to offer suggestions, "Possibly, a virus attached to letters or some kind of mailing advertisement. I know at my mosque, my puja complains about the endless snail- mail advertisements delivered by the postal service., everything from charities, janitorial supplies, event planners, wedding suppliers… For every logistical task needed to operate and manage a church, there's some business trying to profit."

"Yes, that *does* offer some possibilities for contamination, Dr. Siribundo. I recall when the nation was practically paralyzed by anthrax-laced letters mailed to the White House," stated Withers while Snider could be observed listening intently.

A message appeared on the information screen in the bio-4 level lab. The team looked at the screen and glanced at each other. Dr. Snider said, "There it is!" Anthony S. Fauci, M.D., NIAD Director appeared on the screen.

"We need answers! POTUS called this morning and wants an explanation. Rumors are flooding social media. The public fears the worse. More death than COVID! Looting all across the US. We must have answers. The only good news is no one has died since Monday. Whatever the infective agent is, it must have originated at the churches… That is the common clue. Our fear is the first responders have been infected and it is just before it spreads throughout the south. We do not know what the next twenty four hours will bring!," Fauci declared.

Dr. Snider responded, "Yes , sir we're on it!"

After a long silence. Dr. Snider responded, "Dr. Siribundo. Why don't you compile a list of all possibilities? Include all mailings the churches received and look for similarities...and we need to do it quickly. Some social media sites are exhibiting signs and language predicting mass suicides. We must find an explanation before public panic gets irreversible. In addition, we must fully equip the three mobile labs. Double-check equipment and inventory: materials we'll need for the investigation: swabs, vials, syringes, sterilized packets of silicone gel for collecting cultures of specimens. Most importantly, we must have extra sealed bio-4 hazard suits. Each of you inspect your own suit to prevent contamination. Make sure your suit is not damaged; you must do a pre-check! Protocol! Breathe for two minutes using the self-powered, air-purifying respirators and make certain there is a complete seal on your hoods. Until we know more about this virus, we have to take all possible precautions to insure zero accidents. In the event that this damn thing is airborne-transmitted, make sure your SCBA system is fully functional and operating perfectly. I can't afford to lose any of you! Once we have checked the mobile labs, the vans will be loaded on C130's. We are fighting against time, folks. Once in the air, you need to give clear, detailed instructions to your team. The plane ride will give you one to two hours to discuss the plan and give your members instructions and answer any questions they may have. Our investigation of this outbreak has to be very much like the investigation of a crime, consisting of detective work, following every plausible hunch and clue while carefully collecting evidence. In forensic epidemiology, our criminal is the bug. Find the bug...how it gets into humans... how it's transmitted. But it's not just the bug we're dealing with; it's people we are dealing with, and in this case, many rural churchgoers who can frequently be rather ignorant, and therefore prone to panic and be victims of misinformation. Also, we need to divide and conquer by conducting as many interviews as possible among any church members who appeared to have the symptoms. Hopefully, we'll find survivors.

He turned to his colleagues, "Pack! I think its best that we divide and collect information. Dr. Withers, you take a team to Boone. I'll organize my team and inspect the Atlanta church. Dr Siribondu, you venture to Virginia. Ground zero has to be somewhere in the churches. Our only lead! We will update each other tomorrow morning. We need investigations at the churches, simultaneously. Withers and Siribondu you need to get our teams to the C130's waiting at Atlanta International. We'll use the internet to *Zoom* tonight at eleven. Be prepared to brief the Surgeon General with your findings."

CHAPTER 10
MT ZION

"Whoa Bucephalus! What are all these people doin here?" Dalton surprised by the crowd in such a remote location. He looked back at the others, "We are a least 20 miles in the backcountry!"

Wally, the last rider in the posse, "What people?" His line of sight blocked by the other riders. Mike stood up in his stirrups and stretched his neck. "Durn there are at least fifty people and twenty tents!"

Dalton surveyed the mob of campers. "I don't see any guns. Many are sitting around the campfire." His horse continued on the path and moved into the strangers' camp. Mike, it's a mix of old and young people. The kids are hanging out with the parents, the kids look frightened about something."

"Should we go around them?" Mike said suspiciously.

"I don't know," replied Ed and Dalton simultaneously.

"Maybe they need our help?" Wally added with concern instead of suspicion.

Dalton brought Bucephalus to a stop; turned around in his saddle faced the others. "Maybe Wally's right. Let's stop."

Wally and Ed jumped out of their saddles and tied the horses off to a Rhododendron bush. Mike as he got off the horse, Queen Silver began to gallop down the trail. Mike had one foot in the stirrup and his right hand on the saddle horn. Positioned on the side of the horse, he yelled "whoooa, whoa! Awe no!! ," fell off and rolled into the cold stream. The horse stopped, looked back and whinnied at Mike on the ground. Some people in the camp were dumbfounded; waited to see if Mike was not injured. Others began to laugh immediately.

Dalton used this mishap to break the ice. "That's our stunt rider Mike everybody." Generated more laughter from the group of strangers, a few elders were not smiling. In fact, in fact they had suspicion over their wrinkled faces.

A few teenage girls looked at each other and giggled. Mike faked a smile, turned turnip red and stroked his pants to remove the water from his soaked wranglers. Sitting on the ground, he took off his boots as he turned them upside down water rushed out. Wally and Ed laughed and shook their heads with big grins.

Although the stunt broke the ice, the men and women in the crowd became uneasy. The elders seemed apprehensive. It was obvious to the boys, there was something more than a friendly recreational gathering. Three men on the perimeter pumped their shotguns and loaded the chamber. The boys shocked and did not know what to expect next. Dalton said," Hey, let's not get crazy here. We will be on our way. We want no problems. Guys, lets go! Turn the horses around! We just stopped to see if you needed assistance."

A tall graying man stood up. He greeted the boys and ran interference between the giggling girls. He looked back at his wife with a stern face. His bottom lip jutted out under his heavy gray beard. "Young men, what are you doing here? Are you escaping the epidemic too? Or are you goin to Zion to meet the Lord Almighty"

Somebody in the crowd said, "Shoot them! They might have the virus!!"

"What?!" Mike became terrified and feared for his life his eyes were wide open. His mouth was shaped like an "O." Adrenalin pumping throughout his body he gave a fleeting look to Ed. Both the boys thinking to themselves, *we are gonna die.*

Wally not focused on the threat exchange but distressed by the shocking news, "What epidemic?"

The man with the gray beard scanned the group and made eye contact with what seemed to be their leader. "Pastor Phillip, these young men don't know."

Pastor Phillip followed up and moved closer to the boys, "How long have you been on the trail?"

"We started on Sunday afternoon on May 22. We started at Edinburg Gap. Why are you folks here in the middle of nowhere? There are many campgrounds closer to the roads? You must have hiked two days to get here."

"Actually, it took us 24 straight hours. We only stopped briefly. Each time we tried to set up camp more people came. Everyone is fleeing for his or her lives. When we hastened from our homes, 1250 people had died in Atlanta, 650 or so in Boone, and the last we heard 274 in Central Virginia. Actually, close to here." Pastor Phillip responded in a sympathetic manner and tone. "One Sunday, people have died all over the Southeast. Thousands!"

"The victims are all Christians!" The gray bearded man's wife added with trepidation in her voice.

Many of the campers uttered. "IT'S RAPTURE!" Indistinctive chatter began. Quiet whispers and Bible verses began in a chorus chant from the individuals. "Their voices rose in unison, "Praise Jesus! he has come back as the Great Warrior. Judgment is upon us!"

One child asked the pastor, "Are these the four horseman from Revelations?" Nearly star struck.

Ed chuckled, "No, we just four horseman taking a trail ride after graduation." Dalton, Wally and Mike laughed and smiled at the little boy.

"What's your name, little guy? Sounds like you know your Bible. Never thought about it before, but we do have a pale, red, black and white horses." Wally laughed even harder.

Mike looked at Ed, "What's Wally talking about now?"

An elderly woman in a long dress with a dark scarf wrapped around her neck opened her Bible to John 3:16. Put her finger on the red letters moved two inches from Dalton's face. "Are you reborn in the blood, boy? His blood will make you white as snow. Do you accept Christ as your savior? Say yes now, repent boys! He's coming for us! Join us to meet him on this here mountain top. Do you know the name of this mountain, boy?"

"Yes, it's called Mt. Zion." Dalton trembled.

"This is our gate to heaven, boys!!" The elderly woman shook her index finger at Mike. "I'll be sitting with Jesus soon! My blessed redeemer." Others in the crowd shouted, "Amen!"

Wally's eyes became wide. He studied the crowd and as many nodded in affirmation. The devout folded their hands and prayed. Some began to dance in the spirit.

Dalton rolled his eyes and blinked, threw his hands up, "Unbelievable! Oh, here we go! I bet that elderly women goes out-slain in the spirit."

Wally looked back at his friends. His Adam's apple appeared to travel from his chin to his chest. He turned his head away from the crowd. "Hey what's a matter with his fetlock, Dalton?"

"Wally, I don't see anything."

Wally bent down and slid his hand down Cooper's right front leg. The pale horse responded and lifted her hoof off the ground. Wally used his hoof pick to begin cleaning her frog. Wally looked at his friends, "I think those folks think we are in the beginnings of Biblical tribulations."

Mike joined the two, "What? These county people are lunatics, bunch of country hicks."

"You know Revelations and stuff!" Ed responded to Mike's comment.

Wally nodded his head, "Yea, that's it."

CHAPTER 11
TRIPPED UP

Snider's team left the CDC headquarters and drove through metropolitan Atlanta. All major news networks had released the tragic events. The tone was not as shocking as 911, but that many people dying in this event did once again horrify the public. Dr. Snider's team arrived at the church. Military vehicles surrounded the church campus. MP and police officers heavily armed, guarded the perimeter of the Atlanta mega church. A crowd of upset and anxious family and friends of church members tried to penetrate the blockade. Each individual in the crowd feared the worst news of their love ones. No one was allowed to go into the church.

The sliding door of the mobile biohazard van, marked with the CDC emblem, opened. Dr. Snider stepped out from the passenger seat. His highly specialized team exited behind him carrying HAZMATcollecting equipment in backpacks. Inside the van, hung the yellow HAZMAT suits. Taking a deep breath and looking briefly at the deepblue Atlanta sky, Snider, said to himself, *"I hope I find an answer to what caused this death."*

Dr. Snider then ordered his HAZMAT team, "Let's go through the equipment checklist one more time: swabs, vials, syringes, sterilized packets of silicone gel, liquid nitrogen container," to which his chief crewmember replied, "check" each time.

"If we find this virulent agent, it must be shipped frozen. Any degradation in the sample will ruin our chances of solving this case. We want the bug preserved and ready to transport to the CDC Lab. The last thing we want is an equipment mishap," Snider finished with an acknowledging nod from his technician. Snider gave the order, "Suit up!" Each member of the team began putting on their hazmat suits; a process that required utmost care and precision.

The hazmat suits were made of a distinctive bright yellow material, its crinkly texture indicating its protective properties. Reinforced with multiple layers, designed to shield the wearers from hazardous materials and harmful substances. The team members proceeded with a calculated methodology, ensuring that every inch of their bodies was entirely covered and protected.

First, they slipped on long sleeves, followed by snug-fitting gloves that extended to their wrists, ensuring not a single patch of skin was exposed. The gloves were impenetrable, providing a secure seal that prevented any external agents from breaching the suit. Each glove secured with an airtight seal around the cuff, leaving no room for even minute toxic particles to enter.

Next came the upper body protection, a jacket-like garment that sealed tightly around their waists and necks. It had a zippered front, reinforced with a Velcro strip offered an added layer of protection against potential leaks. Members painstakingly pulled the integrated hood over their heads. The protective hood piece completely covered their faces with only their eyes peeping through the clear face covering.

The team now protected, began their walk to the church's front doors. As they took each step, the minds focused on the proper HAZMAT protocol. Each hoped that their efforts would reveal the toxin or maybe the person behind this evil act. After the long stroll in their gawky and obstructive suits, the team was challenged by negotiating the concrete staircase. The investigators reached the outside entrance of the church. The area was a beautiful large marble portico. One member pulled open the large heavy door, and held it for the others to follow. One by one, they stepped into the vestibule of the church. The welcoming foyer was silent and had a ghostly feel. Just hours ago, the greeting space was filled with visitors and congregants sharing loving conversations; each member of the congregation had prepared to leave the burdens of the outside world and enter the sanctuary of the church's worship area. One of his team members flipped the light switch. As Dr. Snider began his observations, he noticed raincoats and colorful umbrellas filled the beautifully handcrafted wooden storage units; each an item left behind by an unfortunate victim. The bulletin boards had informational displays of future events: baptisms, chorus practice, mission trips… All the investigators thought how the hope and joy of Christ like outreach came to an abrupt and mysterious end; to them it made the space feel as a funeral parlor; not in a church.

Snider told his collecting agents, "Begin making your collections in this foyer. Probability tell us that all the folks or nearly all the victims passed through this area of the complex. Investigate and search every possibility of a human contact. The team looked at each other, the least experienced technician speaking through his muffled communication system, "A needle in a haystack."

Snider smirked, "Nobody else in the world could find this proverbial needle. So, let's do this!! In the meantime, I'm going to inspect the sanctuary. "

"Got it, Doc," the team replied unanimously.

Snider stepped though the carved mahogany double doors and entered the sanctuary. The atmosphere was tranquil and reverent, the décor designed to foster a sense of spiritual devotion and worship. Ambiance balanced the illumination and hushed intimacy on beautiful artwork displayed by the giant stain glass window behind the pulpit. Light from outside radiated through the mosaic of Jesus carrying a single lamb. The spectrum of hues shining through highlighted the artwork on the walls added emphasis to the displayed frescoes depicting biblical portraying events such as the Crucifixion, the Last Supper, and from the life of Jesus Christ.

Stepping down the pew aisle his inspections of the sanctuary interrupted by a stumble. Catching himself by the nearby pew, he looked down to realize, Snider tripped over a victim. The male in his forties had his baby in his arm reaching for the door that Snider had just passed through. The victim had dark circles around his eyes that bore a silent testimony of witnessing such unspeakable horror. Every facial crease and wrinkle provided evidence of what took place in the sanctuary hours before. His dilated, fixed pupils revealed his impending death. Just a quick glance, Snider got a shimmer of the horror all the victims experienced.

His mind began questioning the tragedy; someone has a deep vengeance against this church and most likely the other attacked churches. It would seem a hatred towards Christianity. Some criminal minded demonstrated pure evil to attack a harmless place such as this and defenseless people. Dr. Snider blinked, shook his head, and thought, I need to focus on the job at hand. How did it happen?

CHAPTER 12
PUZZLING POISON

The three lead forensic epidemiologists returned to CDC headquarters in Atlanta. They gathered in the breakroom room inside their state of the art Level 4 lab; located in the center of the laboratory working space. The glass walls reflected the team as they sat at a table in the biological laboratory located in the basement of the CDC. The laboratory designed for complete containment of lethal contagions. As an additional safeguard, the concrete structure was underground and enclosed by six-foot-thick walls and ceiling. Well lit with LED lights, the working tables were stainless steel. The white tile floors mirrored the blue-tinted lights, giving the lab a somewhat ethereal feeling. The working area of the level four containment laboratory was bustling with activity, as scientists in white lab coats scurried from one workstation to another. The constant hum of machines filled the air as the team prepared to discuss a new and urgent case.

The rendezvous was within the confines of the breakroom. The three forensic epidemiologists were ardent to compare collected data from each site. Communication of the instrumental information was vital to tackle the challenges of the tragedy at hand. The glass walls provided a sense of privacy and allowed them to focus on the task without any distractions. The meeting space the brilliant epidemiologists occupiedused for coffee breaks and lunch, but for now it was to share critical information. Their main objective was to collaborate and devise a plan to identify the source of the outbreak and develop effective control measures.

Dr. Withers rubbed her eyes with both hands. She was sleep deprived getting back from her investigation in North Carolina. She began her report with pictures of the scene on the large monitor. Dr. Withers used the system as an extension of her hands. She was a wizard with technology. She had spent her life searching information, delivering and educating others. The size of the audience did not matter if a small groups or full auditoriums. She was a master presenter. A touch screen was on podium surface, which mirrored the monitor behind Dr. Withers.

She made eye contact with her peers and she manipulated the touch screen. Each picture illustrated the same horrified faces as the Atlanta development and depicted how each victim came to a painful quick death. Each victim's face disclosed a dismaying demise. As the pictures appeared on the screen, the other epidemiologists said to themselves. *I saw that too.* With a facial expression of agreement, Siribondu nodded.

Snider recognizing the similarities, "It's evident that these cases are interconnected. The parallel patterns and characteristics strongly suggest that they are linked to the same group or individual."

Withers responded to her colleague, "Yes I agree. My team counted five hundred ninety eight dead and only three adult members survived inside the sanctuary. We observed bodies in varying positions. Some positioned with arms laid stretch out and relaxed. We moved their extremities, arms and legs had total flexibility. "Ragdoll" if you will. The death rate must have been slow almost putting them to sleep. However, others examined had no flexibility and I infer they died in total anguish. These victims were crawling towards the door. I would conjecture they knew death was immanent and were trying to escape. We took samples from everything that had human contact. Blood samples are frozen and ready for serological testing."

Snyder nodded his head and then turned his focus to Siribondu. She was already on her feet walking towards the podium. Withers walked back to the table sitting across from Snyder. Dr. Siribondu changed the screen. In view was the picture of the country church in Virginia. On her first slide, the others saw state police officers in airtight masks connected to air tanks on their back. Virginia state HAZMAT unit suited up for the worst in their protective gear. She continued to her next screen. This frame exhibited a close image of a dead rattler lying across the back pew. Blood from the snake was still dripping from its head.

Snyder's eyes grew wide, astonished, "Well, that's different than my site."

Dr. Withers out of character, "What the heck?"

Dr. Siribondu, "I knew this would be your reactions and why I started with this slide. I can explain. This church is Pentecostal. Handling the vipers shows people of greater faith. If filled with the Holy Ghost provides them with the spiritual gift to control the evil creatures of the earth- the snake in the Garden of Eden. You know back to Adam and Eve. In fact, I spoke with one elderly man that stated in the interview, *"They will pick up snakes ... and when they drink deadly poison, it will not hurt them at all ..."* (Mark 16:18)

Snider asked, "Were the evil spirits controlled that day?"

"No, we observed a few members with evidence of snakebites, but not all the dead had venomous punctures. We noticed that the snake bitten victims were all located up front, near the pulpit."

Snider stated, "The Bible also says, Jesus's response to Satan in the holy city was, *"You shall not tempt the Lord your God."*

Dr. Siribandu pointed at her monitor with her index finger slightly curved, her eyes wide, and her attention totally focused on the screen. Almost tearing up, she added, "Many of the congregation were outside huddled together, in fact, many positioned on top of each other. The man I interviewed said, *"The groups were praying for the others inside."* He watched each one drop to the ground. It must have been horrifying watching his friends die. He described, each trying to breath and total fear in their eyes. I almost believed him when, *"he stated it is the work of the devil."* Her expression filled with compassion. Wither nodded her head.

Snider stated with command, "We must keep the emotions out of the scenario. The answer is in the hard data, which we have trained our entire adult life to trust." The session was about to end and the lab serological testing to begin. He summarize the information collected,

"We must work with what we know and this is what we have gathered thus far. Death was within one hour of the services starting. It took some time for each victim to succumb to whatever. It would seem they were conscious; evidence from the consistent emotional eyes indicates that. The body positions and locations are a mystery, similarities but... Our collections would suggest less than five minutes when the onset of toxins or bug took over their bodies. Comparing the quantitative survivorship evidence, seven percent, ninety-three percent of the individuals died. Some pathologic maniac used a powerful lethal substance, but who, what, why and our job, how?"

CHAPTER 13
BIG OLE PARTY IN HEAVEN.

The young men came to the end of the day, just around sunset when they arrived at an Appalachian Trail-style shelter, the basic leanto: three sides but open in the front, open to the deciduous forest landscape…and local wildlife. They spent some time, sweeping eaten acorn shells and animal droppings out the front with cut pine branches.

"The damn squirrels coulda cleaned up after themselves!" Dalton grumbled as the others examined their temporary home that looked like three-quarters of a frontier log cabin. The tin roof would protect the campers from rain and morning dew. Their resting spot provided a picnic table and a fire pit and enough space to make dinner as well as the shelter for much needed rest. The fire pit would allow each cowboy to watch the coals burn down in the increasing darkness. They brought their steeds to a complete stop.

Dalton called his orders. "Well, y'all, let's go ahead and dismount an' get'em fed and watered; stake'm here in the field next to the stream…an' let's lead 'em over to the daisy-filled meadow so they can graze. Pound yer stakes in good an' tie 'em off good so they won't wander off. Our mounts need that fresh grass. The feed store's sweet feed don't have the Omega-3 fatty acids!"

Ed and his peers nestled in their sleeping bags after enjoying a warm dinner of trout and potatoes. Mike was focused on the campfire.

"Man, look at it cracklin' away, and throwin' off beautiful sparks in every direction. I really like the glowin' bright orange, with patches of yellow and red mixed in."

"Gee, you're so poetic!" Wally said.

"No, he ain't!" Ed remarked, "Nothin' rhymed!"

"Aah, shuddup!" Wally grumbled.

Mike chimed in, "The lustrous golden flames are reachin' up towards the velvet black sky, full of stars twinklin' above like heavensent lightning bugs!"

"I'm gonna puke!" Wally grumbled some more.

"Agin!" snickered Ed. Mike laughed.

"Let me see ya turn green agin!" Dalton laughed and shook his head. "Told ya not to swaller."

Dalton offered his piece of the relaxing evening, "The aroma of wood smoke, and the cracklin' of the fire is almost hypnotic. It's peaceful. God made evenings like this just for us intrepid adventurers. Do you think Jesus and the disciples ever had an evening like this?"

Wally smiled. "Well, they were mostly fishermen, so I would say yes as they looked at the stars reflected in the sea."

Dalton asked, "Wally, do you really believe that Jesus and Rapture stuff?"

"Well, Dalton, my boy," Wally began, assuming some kind of professor's tone, "I do believe in Jesus, and I do believe that the rapture is gonna happen someday. I can't say for sure when, but I do believe He's comin' and I'm tryin' my best to make sure I'm ready for it when it comes."

"I've read somewhere that there's supposed to be a real loud sound indicating that Jesus has arrived, but what kind of sound do preachers think?" asked Ed.

"Yeah, some preachers believe that when Jesus returns, there will be a loud command, like a trumpet call from God, that will be heard all over the world. This loud sound is believed to be a sign for those who are ready for the return to Heaven, and it will signal the start of the rapture…so, when preachers talk about this loud sound, they're referring to this trumpet call of God."

Mike, churched by his parents his whole life, said. "Well, guys, rapture is somethin' that some folks believe happens when Jesus comes back to take all of His believers away to Heaven. It's like, the world's gonna end, y'all, and He's gonna come on down and take all believers away, like in the blink of an eye. All of 'em that believe in Him and have accepted Him as their savior will be taken up to Heaven, an' the rest will be left behind. It's kinda like a big ol' party in Heaven!"

Ed snickered, "Well, I like parties, I believe!"

"Me, too!" said Mike and Dalton.

CHAPTER 14
STATE OF AGONY

Withers dressed in her white lab coat, used her index finger and thumb to adjust her rimless glasses. The mirror of the monitor screen seen through her blue light blocking lenses reflected the data collected at all three churches to the other epidemiologists. She was always looking at some type of screen: observations on monitors over 50 hours a week, was more than her eyes could take. "What is possibly common among all three churches? All died before the service was over. ..at the same time. I would infer that the contaminant has to be in the churches. Do we know if the thing is airborne? That's my first hypothesis for dispersion."

Siribondu commented, "I agree, contaminated air would provide transmission of the toxin and a mass delivery over each congregation. All victims exposed at the instantaneous interval."

Snider raised his eyebrows, rolled up his sleeves, "Has hazmat thoroughly inspected the H-VAC systems? You remember the Legionnaires."

"The teams have not delivered the samples as of yet. We are anticipating collections sometime tonight." Siribondu informed the other scientist. "I will do a follow-up call. Try to contact the field supervisor to confirm ventilation sampling. The crews are still near each church. If this was a location that was overlooked we will certainly have them on it in the morning!"

Snider looked at his team, "Yesss, let's start from the beginning! We know our number one rule is the people tell the story. The interviews will lead us to hard evidence. The victims will give us strong clues and provide observations to make solid a hypothesis. So, let's talk and review the data we've collected." Dressed in his Miami Marlon's baseball jersey, Snider collected pitcher's jerseys, and one he was wearing was one of twelve. Slapping his hands on the table, he continued, what else do the initial victims share in common? Think: what do people do during church services, no matter the denomination? We have to trace everything that happens in a church service. What else did the members have or do in common? All members had to come in contact with the toxin at one location or chronological intersect. Initial contact will be our best clue. The chronological intersect between them all is our biggest clue!"

Dr. Withers muttered, "How can three congregations all die at the same time in three different states?" Could this be a coincidence?"

"Aah, come on, we all watch NCIS, You know what Gibbs says. No such thing as a coincidence," Tristan Snider shook his head.

"What about the health care reports? This information is coming in at a very fast rate. Let's match some common data among all three localities." Siribandu, dressed in a blue blouse that had a milk stain from feeding her baby. Self-conscious about the dirty shirt, she looked at the team members, "Sorry, the baby burped on me, and I did not have time to change."

Snider smiled warmly, "Aaah, the sign of a good momma!"

She rubbed at the stain and then continued, "Let's see, in all three congregations the victims, although miles apart have the same infirmities: the living witnesses interviewed stated; confusion in the early onset, people grabbing their chest, fainting, foaming at the mouth, severe seizures,m and then a painful death. All the victims were blue with venation and extremely stiff. First responders noticed premature rigor mortise in some and others like rag dolls."

"That's weird!" Withers made a startled face, "What could cause that?"

"Jeez, whatever it is, turned them into zombies! It's happening, the zombie acropolis," Snider trying to stir some humor and soften the room's tension, speaking to so much death.

"It can't be that. They're not going around eating people, yet." Out of character, Withers followed his lead. She giggled.

"Ya all, get real!" Siribondu moderately upset by her colleague's mockery and absurdity, "What toxin could initiate rapid riga mortise? Chemical or biological?"

Withers turned her head away from Snider. The reflection of her monitor appeared again in her glasses. "That's the big question. Chemical or biological?"

One hour later each team met in the middle of the lab and compared findings. "Nothing seems biological," stated Dr.Siribondu. Still in the confines of the head dress. Each statement was short and difficult to hear by the muffled sound of the breathing system.

"Yes nothing resembled – bacteria or mycota," Withers responded and supported Siribondu findings.

"Yes, we concur, no indicators of nucleic acid. No mRNA or DNA," Siribondu responded to Withers with an added nod as her chin slowly moved down to her lower neck.

Dr. Withers began to analyze, "Whatever the contaminant, it alters the rate of metabolic demise. The deterioration of actin-myosin complex is accelerated. The strands of muscle are binding faster. Almost immediately. The reports indicate that the victims were stiff by the time first responders made it to the scene. At room temperature, it should be; after death, aerobic respiration in an organism ceases, depleting the source of oxygen used in the making of adenosine triphosphate. At normal room temperatures, this should be a 4-8 hour change."

Snider nodded his head and affirming by stating, "Yes, that is our typical pre-autopsy protocol, and we can usually rely on that forensic pattern. Based on the phosphorylation of ADP. ATP is required to cause separation of the actin-myosin cross-bridges during relaxation of muscle. When oxygen is no longer present, the body may continue to produce ATP via anaerobic glycolysis. When the body's glycogen is depleted, the ATP concentration diminishes, and the body enters rigor mortis because it is unable to break those bridges. Whatever the bug or toxin, it is catalyzing the removal of available oxygen."

"Well, that gives us something. Not much…"

"What others possibilities can we derive from the interviews?" inquired Withers.

"Well, the severe seizures definitely indicate a destruction of the nervous system. If the metabolic energy systems is destroyed we would see total systemic failures." Siribondu shared her incite.

"That does make sense," Acknowledge Snider. As the team leader Snider broke the discussion to a close, "Physiognomies recorded indicate a state of agony in all victims. Confusion was the first characteristic nearly every observer described to us. No matter which church we all have the same note. It sounded as if the victims were in a total state of horror, if all the systems collapsed, that would certainly send pain throughout their bodies."

CHAPTER 15
CDC TO CIA

"We don't have enough time to run the gambit of tests! Let's forego analysis of the serum electrolytes, blood urea nitrogen, creatinine, blood gases, and urinalysis," Snider commanded his team.

"But that is standard protocol for suspicion of chemical toxins?" questioned one of Siribondu's team members. We have always assessed the patient's metabolic status, renal function and overall organ function. How else can we be certain of the kill dosage?"

Withers instructed and assured the team member, "I agree and you're correct, that is standard procedure. This case is not standard, and very high ranking government people are demanding answers. We have to go with the quickest method for identification."

"In our pursuit to identify the cause of the mysterious deaths, we have to use the spectrophotometer. Now, you know how critical it is to be certain and using UV light gives us an undeniable "chemical fingerprint," Snider followed up to reinforce the chronological constraint and the accuracy of identification of the compound.

Wither added, "I think we can hypothesize it is a manmade chemical. All biological agents are highly unlikely to kill in less than an hour. However, this one did. All victims succumb to the toxin before the church services ended. Botulism, bacteria and virus will take at least 24 hours in adults to run its metabolic attack."

"Let's start the chemical analysis first! Ricin has been used in recent times and somewhat fits the victim's symptoms. To positively confirm the presence of ricin, we must compare the absorption spectrum from this saved known spectra of ricin. I obtained it from doing some graduate studies at the University. Using my prior recording we identify this thing," Withers glanced at her notes from years past and instructed her technician to set the wavelength controller between 400nm to 100nm. Run the samples now! We are looking for a spike at 340 nanometers. This will identify the ricin." Withers said hurriedly and confidently.

"Yes, Doc. On it." The technician pulled her pipette out of the sterilized cabinet and connected the 5mL green tiny tip. She then slowly slid the tip into the serological sample from the Atlanta Church and removed 5mL from preserved sample. The tech moved the pippete over the crystal clear cuvette, designed to fit into the compartment of the spectrophotometry. She delicately pressed the plunger. The deathly sample filled the cuvette.

Dr. Snider commented, "Well done. Let's see what we got."

The Spectrophotometer screen instantly showed a curve. Across the bottom was the nanometer recordings; the scale 100um to 400nm was projected to where all team members could see. Each scientist studied and knew what they were looking for; the use of this machine was common as a pen in the biological laboratory. The spectrophotometer worked by using a light beam, typically in the ultraviolet-visible range, to pass through the sample solution. As the light passed through, the instrument measured how much light was absorbed at different wavelengths. Each toxic compound, has a unique absorption spectrum, which allows for their identification. If their findings aligned with the characteristic absorption pattern of ricin, it would serve as a crucial piece of evidence pointing to the compound as the cause of the deaths.

Snider commanded, "Put it on the screen! It's not a match. The signature 340 nm spike is absent. However, that's the bug that did the souls in. This is an attack and a mass murder. What is it? Withers check your notes! Do you have something that has a spike, drop, and spike?" Withers fumbles through her black hard covered lab book. She turned the pages quickly. Muttering, "No, no… Wait! Here's one seventy five percent at 200nm, ten percent at 225nm and ninety percent at 260nm."

"Withers, what is it?" asked Siribondu.

"It's one of oldest killers, Strychnine!!"

"Put together a briefing now!! Forward a screen shot, so I can show it to the brass!!" Dr. Snider raced to the locker room.

Withers and Siribondu right behind Snider entered the breakroom. Snider said, "are we ready?

"Okay, okay, let's make the call. We are a go! Got everything those boys will need. God knows we can skip the details. I don't have eight hours to explain it all to them," Withers rolled her eyes and scoffed.

"Always a know it all. Beat the boys," Smiled Snider.

On the other end of the line was David Lindley, Principal Deputy Director at the CDC, spoke rapidly into the phone with obvious agitation, "Snider what do we have? Is the south facing a deadly epidemic? My understanding is attacking the nervous system. How long are victims living once they've been infected?"

Dr. Withers responded, "Sir, people are dying in less than an hour. Convulsions, erratic behavior, loss of balance...and all suffering severe systemic pain...screaming in pain until the end. Emergency-room doctors are reporting; victims are showing up dead. Once ingestion occurs, it takes over all major organs. There have been no survivors! Dr. Siribondu says that COVID is the common cold compared to this toxic beast! We have identified the toxin! Strychnine!"

Snider and others disappeared from the screen and showed the absorbance pattern. While the brass looked at the screen, Snider stated, "We have an attack! This is a terrorist strike on civilians. Somebody, individual or group aimed at Christians. The commonality all Christian churches!"

Siribondu, "Satan's spawn!"

Dr. David Lindsey stated, "No longer epidemiology, this is militant! Home Land Security, CIA stuff now. I'll make the call."

Lindley responded, "You have a short list of military internal physicians specializing in the transmission of toxins. We have a small unit because of cuts by Trump and now a few by Biden. Fools! How do you cut a budget rolling off COVID!?"

Lindley added, "However, one team has never been financially cut! A specialized group working with top brass and the CIA. Since the COVID pandemic, they've been following and analyzing potential biological threats. The funding never stops. Open bank account! Many biological attacks halted by tracking equipment and chemical supplies. They audit scientific supply companies. Some of the agents are undercover as IRS agents. Money is like cheese; it leads us to the rats."

"That's great, but money is not what killing people is," Mocked Dr. Withers.

"But wait, let me finish," said Lindley. "The top person in our organization is Dr. Dean Walesy, an army doc who's been researching weapons of mass destruction before COVID and the Yme virus," replied Lindley, putting down the phone and looking in his file drawer, pulling out Dr. Walesy's contact information, "Turn on your team's monitor, we need to have a Zoom meeting." He immediately dialed a number on his second desk phone and then turned on the large monitor at the end of the long conference table.

After two rings, a male voice, deep and resonant, answered. As those in the room stared at the monitor, a man took off his hazmat helmet, a tangled nest of black unruly hair appearing from inside the protective head piece. "Hello, here I am, Walesy, the Doc of Destruction," he announced, almost cheerfully. Simultaneously shedding his hazmat suit. The CDC specialists observed their colleague's dark five-o'clock shadow and a bright-red satin Boston Red Sox jersey.

"He's an expert?!" Dr. Siribondu whispered, opening her eyes wide, looking at Snider and Withers.

Walesy continued in that happy, cheerful voice. "My motto is *always ready to save the human race. Speak your disaster!"*

Dr. Lindley responded, "Lindley here, here with Snider, Withers, and Siribondu. We have a Code Red. This is real. We need the best in the business."

"We've been watching the news and waiting for the call. My squad is ready. Dr. Snider, I followed your team's work through the Yme virus. We're committed to supporting your team. What do you have so far? Any workable hypothesis or epidemiologic observations?" Inquired Walesy.

"This is the worst we've seen!" Snider assured him in a tone that was far from cheerful...or optimistic.

"Okay," with a nod, Dr Walesy replied, looking around at his team gathered in his USAMRID lab, each of his comrades leaning forward attentively and sitting in metal folding chairs. In the background, beyond a large stainless-steel table were Asian viral-distribution maps mixed in with a collage of U.S. Army recruiting posters.

Dr. Snider continued, with obvious urgency in his voice. "Strychnine! I know Home Land Security has feared this since the J-6 event. Strangely, it appears to be targeting Christians in the Southeast."

"Yes, from the nightly news, we heard about those three churches," responded Walesy.

Withers added, "We can't find any clear connection to a group, but it's one of the oldest biological weapons."

Dr. Snider added, "Those two churches are located in good-sized cities. But strangely, one is in a very remote community in Virginia."

"What else is your team doing?" Walesy asked. Responding quickly. As Dr. Siribondo observed Dr. Walesy. recalling what she had heard about this man, and in the heat of the moment, she witnessed his concern and brilliance, and felt assured that he was going to be a part of what she felt was soon to be a all-out man hunt!"

"We have been looking at companies that service churches." Siribondu stated, hoping that she offered a piece of information that could tie a group of vigilantes to the mass murders.

"What kind of services?" Questioned Walesy.

"Smart thinking, Dr. Siribondu! Central location for contamination and then dispersal. I can see why you're one of the best." Walesy's praise brought a smile to her lips, and she actually blushed a little.

"Our team has specialized in toxins, we've have been working on leads from the FBI. Small domestic terrorist groups are showing threats of a biological nature, identified by purchases they've made. Only a few companies produce the materials and instruments to necessary to produce these toxins for bio-level attacks. Following the money trails has helped, according to the FBI."

"Well, like my hero Underdog, 'Never fear, Walesy's here!" Dr. Withers looked at Dr. Snider with an expression that indicated wonder and doubt, *"Is this guy serious?"*

CHAPTER 16
A CHILD IN TENNESSEE

Turning off the large monitor, Withers looked at Siribondu and said, we need to suit up and get back to work! We have nothing at this point to indicate where the contamination took place. We need to sort through the samples and determine how someone could containment a substance that parishioners had contact with.

Clad in their blue containment suits, their dedication and passion for their work was evident as they methodically prepared for their lab session. They were both silent and focused on suiting up to enter the bio Level 4 lab. They completed their final checks, they nodded for acknowledgment of each's readiness to begin their scientific quest. As they stepped into the working space, the air rushed out of the dressing locker room into the working space. Both cleared the HAZMAT threshold, they heard the closing of the sliding air tight door.

Safely confined by the blue suits looked at the array of specimens marked and taken from each church. The two female scientists were back in the bio-4 lab, "Now that we have the victim's symptoms, we need to determine the activities that are commonalities among the three churches. What could it be?"

Withers and Siribondu systematically prepared themselves for hours of rigorous biological and chemical exploration.

Already in the biohazard laboratory space, four technicians prepared the serological samples; clearly labeled with name and church location. Wither's stated, "I'll pull and start the samples with all ages over forty. Leoni, your team work the samples under thirty nine."

The two teams comparison of data was interrupted by a urgent cry from Dr. Snider, "It was nine O'clock Monday morning." Both Siribondu and Withers were startled and eyes wide open. Their faces expressed the same thought. *"Snider never gets this alarmed."* Fear rushed through their minds. *"Do we have a breach, do we have another outbreak?"*

"What's goin on?" One of the technicians said to her superiors, Withers and Siribondu. Withers shrugged her shoulders, and shook her head back and forth. Completely baffled, all six blue fitted specialist made a bee line to the locker room. Each followed protocol to the letter; no urgent matter would eclipse their extreme biohazard precautious and procedure exiting the bio 4 lab. Toxic containment was drilled in their heads since the day each were hired. They dealt with national security and safety every day. Finally, twenty minutes passed both teams made it to the break room where Snider anxiously awaited.

Very confused, Withers blurted out, "What's wrong Tristan? You never get this shook up about cases. Did we have a system breakdown or worse!?"

"No, no. I just got word of a little boy died in a church in Tennessee. The emergency room doctor called to inform me that the child drank a small amount of a communion juice. The doctor stated that his mom cleans the Tennessee church in Nashville, I think. The doctor explained that the juice came from one of the manufactured prefilled communion cups. The little boy took one tiny sip of the juice. His mom stated that he foamed at the mouth had a brief convulsion. She called 911, and he was gone by the time paramedics arrived."

"Oh no, someone has tampered with the communion cups!!" Said one of the technicians on Wither's team.

"Wait! We do not know that. We have no data or evidence to support that hypothesis. The little boy's death could be an isolated event. Tennessee is a long way from our sites in questions. You know the game, we do not want to create undo public fear until we are 100% certain. The Nashville local news is probably already at the emergency room covering the story." Snider continued, "One of the nurses told the reporting doc that the mother put a message on Facebook. The whole town already knows about his death. Of course, with the tragedy from yesterday, people are acting out of fear. Total panic is beginning. We have to find the truth ASAP.

"Did the HAZMAT units collect the trash from each church?" Snider asked.

Withers replied, "Yes, but we have been focused on the serological samples extracted from the victims."

"Well, I believe," Siribondu accentuated, "we still need to work on the victim's bodily fluids. The substance has to be in their cells."

"Yes, I agree, but narrow your focus on chemical toxins. Let's suit back up and get in the lab. Have the technicians pull up absorbance patterns on ricin. Domestic terrorist have access to that stuff." Snider announced with authority.

Withers gritted her teeth and clenched, "this evil act demonstrates a desire for power and control at the expense of others. Who are these bastards?"

"Contact Walesy!! It's the prefilled communion cups!!"

Snider said, "well, in the last days the Bible says Matthew 10:21: *Brother will deliver brother over to death, and the father his child, and children will rise against parents and have them put to death.* Domestic terrorist report this in many manifest posted on the net. God only knows, what's next?"

CHAPTER 17
NEXT TIME HE COMES

"My butt is sore, Dalton, when's the next stop?" whined Ed.

"Boy, you'll just hafta get some calluses on your tushie. Ya'll be a-rite."

In similar agony, Mike asked, "Does your bottom itch? "As he rubbed, back and forth on the English saddle.

"Not mine, no!" Ed said with a laugh, "Why, does yours?" he put his fist over his mouth and snickered, recalling that Mike had used poison sumac to wipe his butt earlier on the trail.

"Yeah, it's drivin' me crazy...an' it's beginning to burn 'cause I'm sweatin', too." Almost with tears in his eyes, he added, "I got this durn rash on my fingers, too." As he extended his arm towards Wally, he kept whining, "I can't stand it!"

Wally had some sympathy for Mike, knowing that they still had six hard days left on the trail. "Mike, I got some alcohol pads and cortisone cream in my kit." He brought his horse to a stop, dismounted, and tied the reins to a huge bush.

Following Wally, Mike jumped off his mount and waited impatiently for Wally to pull the remedies out of his leather saddlebag. Wally had barely pulled the first-aid kit out when Mike snatched it from him, searching for the alcohol packet. Finding it, he tore the top edge of the aluminum wrapper off; then he slid his pants and underwear down to his knees, and wiped his cheeks. Instead of the instant relief he had expected, he was attacked by the stinging pain of the heavy dose of rubbing alcohol on broken skin; it was too much when the alcoholsaturated pad made contact with his blistery bottom.

"Aah, Ouch!" Mike screamed, tears began to flow from the pain. Feeling zero relief as the others laughed. Wally held his belly and bent over with uncontrollable laughter. Dalton slapped his knee and fell backwards onto the ground. Ed remained on his horse and just shook his head. Mike, now suffering what felt like flames on his genitals, desperate for relief, ran and sat down in the cool mountain stream, not caring about how soaked his jeans and jockey shorts were getting.. Eyes red, he released a sigh of relief, and continued to splash water between his legs and trying to rub the film of alcohol off his cheeks. Getting their breaths back after laughing at Mike's predicament, the others began to remove the tack from their horses. Each fed their horse treats and a scoop of sweet feed from a canvas feed sack. Ears back, the horses buried their noses into the grain, the last one licking the sack clean. After giving the horses a nice, long water break upstream from where Mike was still sitting and splashing, the boys then staked the horses in the meadow for the night.

Setting up camp had become routine, and then they began to prepare the evening meal. Beef stew was on the menu, warmed and ready for the cowboys in fifteen minutes once they had a good fire going. The meal was devoured in five minutes; then, with hammocks hung, they rested by the fire and began to reflect on the day's events. Dalton said, "Ed, I think we need to keep you and Mike separated. I saw where your horse kept trying to bite his, an' that's a problem that is bound to get worse. Horses always jostle for dominance," Ed just shrugged and nodded in agreement.

Meanwhile, Wally had been searching his phone for the next day's weather, "Tomorrow's weather looks good, cloudy and seventyfive," he announced. The rest of them settled into the comfort of their parachute hammocks and stared to the west as the orange sun disappeared behind the Blue Ridge, Mike commenting on the spectacular hues of orange and blue, which rapidly faded into a total red sky. The transition was unmatched by anything he had ever seen, he remarked. Exhaling deeply, he finished his observations. "Man, God outdid himself tonight!"

"Jeez, speakin' about God, last night tripped me out," said Ed. "Wonder if the crazies got snatched up last night at Mt. Zion."

Wally, shaking his head, offered, "I doubt it. The next time Jesus comes, everyone will know. Ed, the Greek word for that is *harpodso*." The word *rapture* is never even *in* the Bible."

"Huh! Every time I hear about the end of time, people at church say that. Wonder why?" Mike replied a questioning tone.

"Yeah, well, in Thessalonians, Romans, and Revelations in modern translations, we only see "caught up" and "meet Jesus in the air." The word rapture doesn't appear. It's only the modern theologians that have started to use *rapture* to describe the heavenly event."

"Why did you say, 'I doubt it,' Wally?" asked Ed.

"Well," replied Wally, "

"When Jesus comes the next time, there'll be two major physical events that no one can miss. Nobody has witnessed these in recent times, and not last night."

Mike, still scratching, grimaced and said, "I know this verse: *and every knee will bow and know that He is Lord!*"

"Yeah, that's right!" Wally continued, "the first time Jesus came it was slow an' took thirty-three years and for most of the world it was unexpected, even though it was prophesized many times throughout the Old Testament, ya'know; our Lord is coming to the earth to save humanity.' Ages passed before Jesus was born; now, of course, we celebrate Christmas."

Dalton said, "Everybody knows that."

"Yeah, well, the next time He comes, I think it's going to be a flash. Faster than the blink of an eye. an' that's pretty durn fast! There are two signs that make me believe that we ain't in Rapture:

We ain't heard a loud, great shout rollin' across the sky. Even though we're here, deep in the Blue Ridge, we still should have heard Jesus's return in the sky!"

Mike, still scratching but listening intently, said, "But you said *two* things."

"Yeah Mike, I did," Wally replied. "According to Revelations, Jesus and his army of angels will light up the sky. There is no way we or anybody else would have missed a history-ending event like that."

"Not even on the Fourth of July or New Year's Eve?" Ed quipped.

Ignoring Ed, Wally continued. "It's interesting: the first time He came it was kings and shepherds that supposedly followed the star in the east, just that one brilliant star that was a symbol but not all the people in the Holy Land that saw it recognized it as a fulfillment of the prophecy of the son of God's arrival. The next time the sky is going to be lit up, the *entire* sky will reveal his majesty. No matter where you are, according to scripture, you will witness that Jesus is coming to earth to keep his promise. The best part of the Bible and the reason we acknowledge Jesus is because He left us with this promise. We will have everlasting life. No more worries, no more death, no more suffering, an' no more sickness. We are in perishable bodies but He will transform us into a immortal bodies. We all will be just like Jesus after He rose from the grave. We will be immortal. We will be with Him and the saints for eternity. Now *that* is something to look forward to! Those folks at Mt. Zion know this, and that's the reason why they want it to be true. However, sorry to inform them – it's just not happened!"

"Yet!" Dalton said as he turned face-down in his hammock.

Ed got a small grin on his face. Made a little snicker, "I watched the left behind series, why when rapture occurs Hollywood shows everybody's clothes left? Being naked don't seem very holy. I think I would be a little embarrassed if naked girls were flying around me." Ed, smirked knowing well that Wally was going to say something educated.

"You're dumb. When Jesus left the grave He did not take the cloth wrapped around him. Christ had a new body and we will too!"

CHAPTER 18
JOHN WHITE

Dr. Agent Walesy after taking the message from Tristan Snider, "We have to find out where the churches bought the prefilled communion cups? Siribondu was right on! Central contamination."

Without being directly ordered, Agent Holland looked up the company that processes the communion cups. Holland did not bother to go to her desk. She tapped on the Google icon and searched: "Sir, its Titulada Juice."

"Where is this place?"

"Tallahassee, Dr. Walesy." Holland made maintained consistent and respectful eye contact with Walesy.

On the plane to the Titulada Juice Factory, Dr. Walesy's team discussed the plans for the strychnine poisoning investigation. All reclined in plush leather seats of a CIA Leer Jet. The cabin interior was designed to protect top secret material and evidence. Dr Walesy , an experienced operative known for his sharp investigative skills, in the short period of time after speaking with Snider's team of epidemiologist, had assembled a team consisting of top-notch analysts, forensic experts, and field agents. Their mission was identify the person responsible for contaminating the batch and prevent any further harm. Right away, they called the authorities and worked closely with the police to solve the mystery and bring the culprit to justice. Investigators from all around were summoned to gather evidence and launch a thorough interrogation. The accumulation of this task was scattered on the horseshoe shaped conference table of the jet.

Surrounding each agent was technological equipment only seen in national security spaces. Pictures of the Titulada Juice Factory were on the front large screen. The pictures followed the assembly line of the juice preparation process. The presentation started at the loading dock where fresh fruit was delivered. Next showed the pealing and the juicing process. Finally, the last series of slides showed an array of mechanical parts operated by Titulada employees. As Dr. Walesy displayed each visual, he delegated the investigative assignments to his team members. "Work efficiently, and do not miss anything. The smallest clue can make the difference between suspect and conviction!" he commanded. His persona was all business now. The clownish comic hero character had changed to an intense investigative professional. Those around him had confidence he would find the fanatics that murdered innocent people.

"Jaden, let's dig deeper into the manager's background. Although we're certain he is not directly involved, he may have connections or knowledge that could assist our pursuit of the terrorist groups that we have discussed."

Holland, "focus on the employees, we should also gather information about the factory's security measures. Were there any breaches or unauthorized access during the time frame in question? Investigate if any disgruntled former or current employees might have had the opportunity and motivation to tamper with the products."

"Coop, gather all the surveillance footage from the Tutilado Juice and Canning factory during the six-month period leading up to the contamination. We may be able to identify any suspicious behavior or individuals who could be involved."

"We need to be thorough and methodical in our questioning. Look for any inconsistencies in their stories or odd behavior that may raise suspicion. As you investigate each employee, search for any records of unusual or large purchases of strychnine from suppliers and distributors. Credit cards, Venmo or cash purchases. Someone has left a financial trail!"

As the briefing came to a close, each member began looking at their smart phones. Some smiled as the texts they read came from love ones and friends. One of his experts went immediately to the CNN icon on his iPhone. A female news spokesman reported. "The tranquility of Americas Sunday mornings had abruptly shattered as investigation continues of the sinister act tainting communion juice." Trying to ease his mind, he changed to his FOX, PBS and BBC icons. All networks covered the terrorists attack. The news networks interviewed experts. Each scientist, law enforcement and toxicologist information stated was speculative. Annoyed by the miss information he shut his phone off and shook his head; ran his left hand through his hair. In just two short days the terrorist accomplished their objective. Word of the contamination spread like wildfire, causing panic and unrest in the American public. Religious leaders feared that more churches will be targeted. They cancelled on site services in Churches and Synagogues. As his hand held device's screen closed, he felt the landing gear touch the runway.

Dr. Walesy and his team jumped in the Chevrolet Suburban that waited at the airport. They rushed straight to the Titulado Juice Factory. As they stepped inside, the familiar scent of fresh juice was surreal. Although the fresh fruit aroma was refreshing, they all knew the factory was ground zero of the death on that Sunday morning. The detectives were greeted by D.S Titulado, who led them to the assembly line where the tainted juice cups had been filled.

Dr. Walesy closely examined the machinery and the filling process while Agent Allen observed keenly. She noticed a nervous employee named Julian, who was constantly fidgeting nearby. Agent Allen decided to question him discreetly, suspecting he might hold crucial information.

Pulling Julian aside, Agent Allen calmly asked him about his work and whether he noticed anything peculiar happening in the factory recently. Julian's eyes darted nervously, and beads of sweat formed on his forehead. He hesitated for a moment and then tears ran down his face. In between sobs, Julian confessed that he had seen a coworker, John, tampering with the filling station. Where is John? What's his last name?

Julian responded, "White, John White. We have not seen him this week; I had to cover his shift yesterday and today. Not sure where he is? You need to talk to Kyle."

"Okay, Kyle is your supervisor, right?"

"Yeah, he should be in the office or on the floor."

Julian immediately approached Walesy and informed his boss about John White. "Dr. Walesy, I think we might have something that might prove helpful. Can you ask Titulada to page Kyle Gravitt?" Walesy moved across the room and found D.S. Titulada amongst other employees siting in chairs waiting to be interviewed. Mr. Titulada we need to speak with John White."

Titulada responed. "Yes sir. Let me reach out to Kyle Gravitt." Mr. Titulada picked up a floor phone and called upstairs to have Kyle paged. "Send Kyle to the filling station," ordered Titulada.

Without hesitation, Kyle rushed towards the area where all were waiting. Titulada looked at Kyle and then said looking back at the investigators. "They need John White."

Gravitt responded, "Sir he is not in the building and was absent yesterday. No one has seen him since Friday clocking out."

Agent Allen and Walesy made eye contact. It was evident to the bystanders that each knew they had something valuable and needed to act on it. Quickly like a mountain lion on a deer, "Tell me about this guy!"

Kyle Gravitt, spoke openly and confidently, "He is a new hire. He did not talk much, but is an excellent worker. Very intelligent."

"How do you know his intellect?," Asked Allen.

"Mam, he trained faster than anyone we have hired in years. One training and he could complete all tasks on the floor with ease and minimal supervision." Agent Allen eyes showed suspicion. She gently put her index finger over her lips waiting for more information. "We asked him to cover for a deceased employee. We got word that

Steve Turner was killed by a break into his home. The local police ruled it as a burglary; we as a company were shocked," Kyle's face showed grief.

Mr. Titulada stated, "Yes, that's right, we were in a jam that morning. We had a big order that day for the diocese in Atlanta. The Cardinal in the Atlanta diocese had approved the communion cups because of COVID. This would double our business. We had to complete it. We put him on the floor. He had helped Steve Turner the week before."

All investigators looked at each other and silently thought, *"what as asshole, somebody dies and he's worried about sales.*

Walesy demanded, "What is White's address!?"

CHAPTER 19
THE MAP

Supplied with the address from White's personnel file, Agent Walesy led the way as the team of investigators approached an old, seemingly abandoned house under the cover of darkness. The dilapidated building looked as if it had stood vacant for years. Walesy whispered, "Tonight's mission is crucial in uncovering any incriminating evidence related to the use of strychnine or any possible connection to a terrorist group! Be vigilant, but be safe."

With their walkie-talkies activated, the team of experienced agents moved swiftly, making their way through the overgrown yard and cautiously approached the cracked and badly weathered front door. Agents Allen and Holland followed closely behind Walesy, who easily picked the old lock as the team silently entered the premises. The atmosphere in the house was eerie, revealing the passage of time through peeling wallpaper, broken furniture, and layers of dust. Walesy signaled for the team to split up to search every room, every nook and cranny thoroughly. He pointed and whispered, "Allen, go upstairs. Check closets and don't forget the attic hatch. Holland, go through these downstairs rooms and the kitchen. Inspect the closets and look for loose floor boards. I'll head to the basement."

Agent Walesy carefully searched the basement, equipped with a flashlight to pierce through the darkness. The stagnant basement air had a musty smell, but Walesy diligently scanned the area, examining every corner for any signs of chemical containers or hidden compartments. His heart raced as he discovered an unmarked five-gallon bucket with a suspicious brownish residue inside. Suspecting a potential danger, he swiftly pulled out his communication device and urgently called the other agents.

"Allen and Holland, I think I've found something significant," Walesy whispered urgently into his device. "An unmarked five-gallon bucket with an unknown residue. Proceed with caution, but meet me in the basement."

Walesy carefully approached the bucket, assessing the possible risks. With gloved hands, he picked up a small sample of the residue with a sterile swab, securely packaging it for later analysis.

After hearing the urgency in Walesy's voice, Allen and Holland acknowledged the call for help and promptly made their way down rickety stairs where the team regrouped in the dimly lit basement. They knew immediately the crystallized brownish-white powder was strychnine.

Holland said, "I'll call the HAZMAT unit." Walesy nodded.

The team retreated up to the safety of the kitchen and began looking for more clues. "Now, let's look for something that will tie this guy White to a group!" Walesy ordered as he rolled up his sleeves to the elbows. The other members of the team began to empty the house. Stacks of furniture accumulated in the front yard. The once-tall grass and weeds were trampled into paths. The entire house was cleared of furniture and all floors were exposed. As the team looked around the kitchen, all drawers and cabinets were opened. Discouraged after a fourhour, ten-man search, Walesy was frustrated. "There has got to be *something* here!" he muttered, quoting the *Locard Principle. "Every contact leaves a trace, with contact between two items, there will be an exchange." But where is it?"*

"Yes, sir, we know. We'll search again," Allen responded, evidence that she had heard Walesy's whisper.

"Send a group around the property! "Demanded Walesy. "I doubt that he spent much time in the basement. He had to be trained to handle strychnine. Somewhere around this old house has got to be something! Books, magazines, receipts, papers, receipts...

"Yes, sir, we'll start searching the property," replied Holland as she led her team out the back door in the kitchen. In view were an old weathered barn and a small overgrown cemetery, most likely the final resting place of some farmer's buried relatives that once lived on the property. The barn was falling down and rotten oak boards were dangling from the sides; the entire structure was leaning.

Holland said, "One big wind will bring that down. Careful, don't go in, look through the doors and the windows."

The doors of the barn had fallen; directly in front of the barn was a worn area with a fire pit in the middle. Using fallen branches, the team carefully sifted through the ashes where they found fragments of burnt paper. Hoping they were remnants of messages or receipts, the burnt remnants were carefully documented, photographed, and packaged, ensuring the integrity of the evidence for further examination. Holland instructed her field technician to be careful collecting and handling the fragile paper. Even with care, the pieces began to separate. Another technician caught tiny pieces in a forensic container.

"Hey, boss, possible receipts!" Holland called with some excitement, having seen a line of numbers on several pieces of paper."

"Okay. It's something. Folks, let's pack it up. Back to the jet!" Walesy announced. Hours later, Walesy and the team landed at Langley and hurried to their office with their evidence, eager to get their samples to the forensic lab for further analysis where the lab technicians carefully examined the fragments under a microscope. The trained forensic scientists looked for any discernible information that could be pieced together. Dark lettering did appear as Holland had observed.

"Hey, look at this -- a series of numbers" another technician announced. "I only see four. The others I cannot make out. It might be part of a credit card account. We need to send it to Walesy! Now let's run the sample through the spectrophotometer, maybe the spectral analysis will determine the chemical composition of the ink used on the receipts. Let's use the CIA data bank for ink used by chemical supply companies if the card was used for that... It just might I.D. the location through the data bank."

Within minutes, the supply house was identified. *"Defcon Pests in West Virginia. Send it to Walesy!"*

At his headquarters, Walsey looked at his team that he had gathered. "We need all the transactions of *Defcon Pests* in the last six months! It's a small chemical company located in Nitro, West Virginia. Use the four digits that were readable on the receipts to do a search. Now!"

The members of his team looked over the shoulder of the financial analysis expert as he searched the government data base of chemical companies that had licenses to handle restricted chemicals. The agent's fingers were moving swiftly across the keyboard, and at his click of the mouse came a name on the monitor's screen: the account was owned by *Los Pollos Hermanos.*

CHAPTER 20
RATAS PROBLEMA?

Dr. Walesy entered the *Los Pollos Hermanos* Mexican restaurant and the other agents followed. The ambience was casual and relaxed, reflecting the genuine hospitality of Mexican culture. Walesy spotted Pedro, the owner and manager behind the bar, making a margarita. The team moved across the colorful tile floor and approached him. Pedro made eye contact and said *"Como estas amigo? ¿Les gustaría a las jóvenes y bellas damas una cerveza?*

"No, sir, we're working," Holland responded with a genuine warm and appreciative smile, while Walesy introduced himself as a federal agent. To avoid unnecessary stress or anxiety for the owner, he did not disclose that his team was CIA. "We need to speak with you about a financial transaction. We must have access to your records."

Pedro responded, "Please, *Señor*, not in front of my customers," having noticed that patrons were beginning to stare. Walesy agreed and Pedro led Walesy to a quieter corner of the restaurant. "Yes., sir, how can I help you?" his genuine response was not defensive as agents Allen and Holland had assumed he would be and they quickly glanced at each other.

Allen whispered, "My gut tells me this guy's an unlikely suspect."

Once seated, Walesy began the conversation by explaining his reason for being at Pedro's establishment, "Your American Express account was used to purchase a very large quantity of rat poison. In fact, it was strychnine. Why do you need that much rat poison?"

Quickly. Pedro got very defensive. "My restaurant does not have a ratas problema! What are you talking about, mister? This is a five-star restaurant! Rumors of that nature could shut us down!" He got so angry that he stopped speaking in English and got more defensive in Spanish. *"¿Cómo te atreves a acusar a mi establecimiento de tener un problema de ratas?"*

Holland, in her calming voice, shook her head and held out her hands. *"Nadie está haciendo la acusación de un problema de ratas. Aaa."* She gathered her thoughts, reaching back to her high-school Spanish II class as she continued to try to calm Pedro. *"Necesitamos obtener información sobre su tarjeta American Express, comprendes?"*

Although Walesy was not fluent in Spanish, he suspected why Pedro was so defensive. "Let me restate my question, sir. Can we see your records, please?"

Finally understanding the purpose of Walesy's request, he responded by, "Certainly, I'll be glad to cooperate with you. Mariah, please take them to the back and open up our financial records." Turning to Walesy, he added, "I do things, legally, by the book; and you will see for yourself."

To break the increasing tension, Holland said, *"gracias"* with what she hoped was a very warm and sincere smile.

Mariah sat down in front of the computer screen. The office was very small -- almost like a converted storage closet -- and only had space for one other person to stand. Walesy squeezed in to where he could look over Mariah's shoulder. As she pulled up files on the screen to show their financial summary, Walesy directed, "We need the purchase history of your American Express account. We are looking for a transaction with the file name *Defcon Pests*."

Mariah immediately appeared shocked by the name. "That's alarming, sir. We are right now investigating that transaction. Pedro and I have reported that transaction to American Express as a dispute. We did not make that purchase!" In a strong, angry tone, *"Señor*, it was a large purchase and we do not know why it showed on our account last month. We do not use products from that supplier."

Walsey scratched his head, and looked at Mariah, "It was a very suspicious purchase of a large quantity of strychnine, which is designated as a controlled substance. Here's a copy of the purchase order." Walesy presented his evidence, emphasizing that the last four digits of the American Express card matched Pedro's company card. The purchase was made online to *Defcon Pest* in Nitro, West Virginia.

Pedro, standing outside the small office, looking both concerned and confused, denied any knowledge of purchasing strychnine or having any connection to the mentioned evidence. He insisted that there had to be a mistake, as he had never been to Nitro, West Virginia, nor had he made any such purchase online or authorized such a purchase.

Sensing Pedro's genuine confusion, Walesy decided to further investigate the matter to determine if there was any evidence of identity theft or possible hacking of the company's credit card information. "Holland, Allen, identity theft, you think?" Both Holland and Allen nodded.

Allen muttered softly, "Yes," while Holland, agreeing with the suggestion, added, "Seems to be. I don't think this company is in the business of killing people…or in my opinion, have any reason to commit such an evil attack."

Walesy, standing beside Pedro outside in the small restaurant hallway, assured him, "We'll look deeper into the situation and see if there have been any recent incidents or unusual activities that might indicate more connections."

Pedro responded, "Mariah and I have discussed this and we have no idea how someone could have gained access to our account. You know, sir, right now, very little can be done to track down those carrying out cyber fraud. That was what American Express say to me when I call them. Yesterday, they tell me the dispute is still under review…whatever that means. Review by who?"

Walesy, putting a reassuring hand on the owner's shoulder said, "Don't worry, I'll make a call. Thank you for your cooperation. Oh, by the way, I'm hungry. What's your most popular entre here?" Mariah and Pedro smiled. Pedro said, "Order anything on the menu, *¡Tu equipo come, la casa invita!"*

Walesy, his facial expression puzzled, glanced at Holland. Holland with a full grin, informed him, "Good news, we eat for free tonight!"

Twenty minutes later, after a full-staff briefing, Holland, Allen and Walesy sat down in a booth. Displayed around the dining room were large sombreros hanging on the walls and many pictures of bull fights. Holland, after scanning the room's décor, turned back to the others, "I would say this is authentic Mexican food."

Walesy smiled, "Let's eat." As a pile of nachos and bowls of salsa arrived, the three began to review the evidence. Walesy started the discussion, "We need to find who stole the information from their card and how. Is this a cyber-crime or possibly even someone physically here?"

Allen, looking thoughtful, frowned and looked at Walesy, "You know what I thought was strangely unusual?"

"What?" both Walesy and Hollland asked?

"That guy, John White. It just seemed odd to me that he was so easily trained and available."

"Yeah, I recall Mr. Gravitt remarking that he caught on so quick… almost too quick," Walesy added through a mouthful of chips and salsa.

"Maybe we should investigate that home invasion. Maybe it was not a home invasion, after all. Why would someone break in, an' only steal a shotgun but commit murder? Makes no sense!"

"After dinner," Walesy announced.

CHAPTER 21
THE YURT

Each cowboy's face wore the weight of the long day's ride. Their destination was a special night stay in a yurt in the George Washington National Forest In a very remote area, the nicer accommodation was situated to give hikers and trail riders a nice break from the dusty trail, as well as a spectacular view. The National Park Service had designed the structure so each weary traveler would have a chance to enjoy a natural cold shower provided by a nearby waterfall, at the base of which the twenty-foot-high plunging mountain water constantly filled a wide swimming hole, like an oasis in the heart of the dense deciduous forest and the rugged mountains. Surrounding the natural swimming pool, a rhododendron grove offered privacy for anyone who chose to forego clothing. Here, the only sounds that accompanied them were the steady clip-clop of their horses' hooves and the distant call of birds soaring high above.

Wally called out, pointing up, "Look, a bald eagle!"

Mike looked up and said, "Awesome!"

"Man, that's a sight for sore eyes," said Ed.

Wally wondered, "The eagle?"

"No, man, we've been seeing those the whole trip! I mean that yurt just ahead," he responded sarcastically.

Dalton said, "Let's set up a temporary corral for the horses and get dinner on the fire. Time to eat."

Mike said, "Good, I'm hungry."

"After I secure my horse, I'll start the fire," Ed reported. Half an hour later.

"Man that was good. Thanks, Dalton, once again, you made sure this country boy can survive."

Mike said with gratitude. "An' you know how to cook!"

Ed, Dalton and Wally nestled in their sleeping bags after enjoying a warm dinner of trout and potatoes while Mike was focused on feeding wood to the campfire in the stone fireplace. He was still enjoying the night sky, and because Wally had taught him how to identify the constellations and planets; he made it a nightly habit to quiz himself. The others were in bunks inside the yurt just about to fall asleep.

Mike called out, "Hey, what are all those lights down in the valley?" The rest slowly turned toward the open front of the yurt but remained in their sleeping bags. Impatiently, Mike said, "Hey, seriously, come look at this! "

"Dang it. Mike" Ed muttered, rubbing his eyes. "I was already half asleep!" Crawling out, he opened the wooden screen door and said, "Where?"

"Over there, at the base of the mountain to the north," Mike stated. Pointing in the flickering light from the fire. "We're in the middle of nowhere."

Dalton and Wally, now also out and standing beside the campfire. "I don' know." Dalton, who had studiedthe George Washington National Forest maps each day, replied. "Access to that area is either a mountain stream or an old logging road turned into a fire road. Nothing on the maps indicates any place that could have electricity. Let's go check it out!"

"In the dark? On the horses?" Mike questioned.

"No," Wally said quickly. Too dangerous going down the mountain on horseback at night. I don't think that's a good idea.

Besides, we have another long ride tomorrow an' my ass needs its rest."

"Come on, Wally, you scared?" Ed challenged with a dare, all in one short statement.

"Come on, boys, get yer boots on!" Dalton commanded, ignoring Wally's caution.

Unknown to our intrepid adventurers, those strange lights offered an ominous presence. Concealed by thick foliage and towering trees, they were part of a paramilitary compound. Its presence hidden from prying eyes, the compound, exuding an air of secrecy and danger, was surrounded by a high fence, topped by razor wire, its seclusion and presence equally ominous and threatening.

"Holy shit, what is that?!" Ed whispered.

Despite Wally's warnings, the boys crept slowly down the trail, thankful for the full moon lighting the way. Twenty minutes later, as they approached the compound, they could make out a gated entrance in the ten-foot-high fence, guarded by what seemed to be uniformed soldiers who cradled automatic rifles. Silently, the boys climbed on top of a large bolder that looked down beyond the gate.

Inside were several buildings, constructed of cinderblocks. Wally whispered, "Those ain't army or Marine uniforms an' that biggest building must serve as the nerve center or headquarters of the compound. How'd all this shit get built without anyone knowin' it… an' who *are* these guys?!"

As the boys watched, they could see that despite the later hour, the facility still bustled with activity. The militants in view, in similar clothing as the guards', wore red headlamps and were entering the large building. Scattered throughout the compound were additional, smaller mobile facilities, like compact trailers. Ed whispered, "I think this some kind of a military operation."

"Lower your voice, dumbass, and no shit!" Mike hushed Ed.

"Maybe we can sneak in," Mike suggested.

"They got effing guns! Are you serious?!" Ed snapped. "We could get shot!"

Dalton said, "Well, I could use an adrenaline fix...but let's try it."

Wally, out of character, whispered," Aah, shit, It's stupid but.... I'm in."

"Let's go that way," directed Dalton, pointing down below their boulder to a shrub-bordered path on the other side of a hole in the chainlink fence. Sliding down silently, the boys crept closer to the open rear of the large block building and were shocked by what they saw: an array of weapons, ammunition, and tactical gear.

"Damn, what the tarnation is this place?" Wally gasped.

CHAPTER 22
JEEP AND A SHOTGUN

Dr. Walesy, agents Holland and Allen, along with the local sheriff and two deputies, gathered at Steve Turner's home to reinvestigate his murder. Walesy and the investigative team approached the perfectly maintained Cape Cod home. The wraparound porch was inviting with white wicker chairs that matched the shutters. Dr. Walesy rang the doorbell and one of Turner's children answered the door; the little girl yelled "MOM!" Ms Turner, behind the child, asked, "What's this about, Sheriff?"

"I'm sorry to bother you again, but the federal agents need to reinvestigate. They have learned some new info that might lead us to who killed your husband."

Following the local officer's explanation, Walesy politely asked, "Can we enter your home to review forensic evidence?" The deputy walked Holland to the location of the gun case. She carefully examined the case and discovered fingerprints that had been overlooked on the night of Steve Turner's murder. She scanned the prints with her fingerprint scanner and was able to input the scan into AFIS. Immediately, she had a match: *Robert Lee Washington, age 18.* Walesy asked impatiently, "Why is he in the fingerprint data base?"

"Sir, he's applying to the Corps!" Holland spoke without taking her eyes off the handheld device.

Agent Allen and Walesy diligently gathered additional clues and found evidence of a gunshot. Allen noticed a bullet hole in the living room wall that appeared to be the result of a high caliber rifle being fired from outside. Allen quickly prepared the Advanced Laser Trajectory Finder Kit. She turned the lights off in the room and followed the red light. It passed directly through the window opposite the wall. "This bullet penetration is too deep for a pistol." Ballistics was her specialty. The deputy scratched his forehead and was confused.

"Ms. Turner, did you say that your husband was struggling with the suspect when the shots were fired?"

"Yes," she said slowly.

Allen looked at Sheriff Thomas and commented, "In our investigation, we somehow overlooked this bullet hole. We have it recorded there was evidence of only two shots." He glanced back at Ms. Turner. "Did you hear a third shot?"

She responded, "Maybe. I was in a panic. All I could concentrate on was getting my children to safety. Besides, I was in pain. I was grazed by a bullet. It did not even leave a scar. There had to be two! That's what I told the officer in the emergency room."

"I don't think the suspect fired the kill shot," Allen stated with certainty, "Washington could not have made a kill shot from his angle facing Steve Turner. This autopsy report and crime scene pictures show the wound at the back of Steve Turner's head. Our recent collected evidence does not indicate that Washington could have killed Steve Turner from his location during the struggle. In my analysis, the bullet trajectory indicates that kill shot and the wall evidence came from the outside!"

"We need to pick up Robert Lee Washington! Sherriff, where can we find him?" Walesy demanded.

Holland quickly reviewed the AFIS information, "It says he lives at 4418 Packard Street."

One of the deputies added, "That's only a mile and a half from here." Sherriff Thomas ordered, "Pick him up and we'll be at the station waiting for you and the perpetrator."

Walesy added, "Holland, go with them in your car!"

As the small group of deputies and Holland pulled up to the address, a nice-looking young man was getting into a red lifted Jeep. All the officers pulled their pistols and pointed them at Robert Lee Washington.

"Please, do not shoot, I will cooperate ... whatever this is about" he announced. He lifted his hands off the steering wheel. Without a struggle, the two deputies handcuffed Washington and slid him into the back of the white patrol car.

Waiting at the station, Allen had already begun looking into Washington's background. "No criminal record. I called the high school, and he does not even have a tardy. In fact, he has a 3.4 GPA and plays three sports."

"How did this kid get caught up in this?" Walesy wondered, "Somethin's rotten in Demark." Allen nodded in agreement. Just then Holland and the deputies entered the interrogation room and Holland informed Walesy that their suspect had been apprehended. Walesy looked at his phone and said, "We got him!" Minutes later Walesy sat down, face-to-face with eighteen-year-old Robert Lee Washington.

"Son, we have your finger prints at a crime scene. In fact, son, you're a suspect in a murder." Without hesitation, Washington responded, "I broke into the house, but sir, I did not kill Steven Turner! I did not shoot him. I don' know how he was shot. I admit I stole the shotgun. I wrestled with Mr. Turner, trying to get away. He had me in a bear hug and I thought I was caught for sure. Then I heard a shot and Mr. Turner dropped. I swear!"

"Son, why, with your clean record and success in school," Walesy paused put his index finger on his lips, "would you do something as stupid as break into a home and steal a shotgun? The damn thing is probably not worth four hundred dollars!"

"I.I.I donna know!" Washington moaned and began to cry and put his face in his hands. He paused and lifted his face from his hands.

Walesy stared into Washington's red teary eyes. "Robert, you're not telling us somethin.'"

Robert got very anxious and tried to get up from his seat. "You need to sit down, son, and come clean or you're going to prison for murder. That's a very long time for a young man like yourself."

"I know, I know, but I did not shoot a gun that night!"

"If you didn't, then who did? Son, have you ever been on the inside of a prison. I have and you would not do well in there. Why did you break into a home a steal a shotgun, Robert?" Walesy slammed his fist onto the metal table.

The sound startled Robert. "My uncle. He paid me to get it back. He said, if I get his grandaddy's gun back he would buy me a Jeep. He said that Mr. Turner won it in a pool game. My uncle said he cheated him. I thought I was helping my uncle and getting a Jeep, too. I have always wanted a Wrangler, sir."

"You say your uncle!" Walesy glanced over at the two behind the see-through mirror on the back wall. What's your uncle's name and where is he, son?!"

"Michael Washington, sir," the young man showed some relief. "I think he's at work. He's an accountant for Southeast Bank."

Walesy stood up abruptly and shouted, "Sherriff Thomas, Holland, Allen You heard it --"let's go!"

CHAPTER 23
RANTING WASP

Dalton, positioning himself under an opened window just feet away from the man at the podium, signaled to the others by waving his hand behind his back. In his squatted position, he could see the leader clearly.

"Get over here and look at this," Dalton whispered softly. The leader, dressed in green fatigues and a tan Stetson campaign hat, stood at the front of the assembly. The hat had an emblem -- although difficult to distinguish from a distance – of a shiny gold figure; which seemed to resemble a wasp. Following Dalton's signal, the others slid on their bellies to move against the exterior wall of the building. Peering through another window, the boys could see rows of seats, metal folding chairs that the militants were slowly filling. As they entered the building, the men turned off their red head lamps. Each sat down without any conversation and awaited the next command.

Ed whispered, "Wonder what the old Colonel Sanders twin is going to say."

As the meeting was about to start, they were able to see each militant up close. "Damn, this reminds me of a church service on *Duck Dynasty*. Crazy ass white guys with beards. Look, there's Thoreau and Whitman," Ed whispered, then covered his mouth with his fist and snickered.

"Well, hell, there's Clemons and Dickens behind him," whispered Wally.

"Shut up!" Dalton hissed, putting his index finger over his lips. "We don't wanna get caught by these guys. They're some kinda freeakin' right-wing assholes."

The boys heard one of the militants nearest their windows snap, "Quiet" to the man sitting beside him, sporting a black cotton army cap. "Colonel Sanders is about to speak!"

Dalton looked at Ed, "Colonel Sanders?! You gotta be kiddin'." Ed snickered. Mike and Wally seemed totally shocked, their eyes so wide their eyebrow reached their hairlines, and close to having a laughing fit. Dalton followed with a comment that caused even more risk of laughter. "Stop! Colonel Chicken Legs is about to start his speech." The boys put their hands over their mouths prevent any laughter from becoming detected by the troops inside. The elderly man at the podium stroked his long wide beard, put one hand over his heart, then raised it and saluted the over-sized Confederate and American flags behind the podium. When he did, all the uniformed followers stood up and saluted at the exact same time. Not a sound was heard. The leader then turned around and looked at the crowd, dropping his hand. Simultaneously, on cue, the white men in unison chanted: *What we must fight to safeguard the existence and reproduction of our race and our people, the sustenance of our children and the purity of our blood, the freedom and independence of the fatherland, so that our people may mature for the fulfillment of the mission allotted it by the creator of the universe. Every thought and every idea, every doctrine and all knowledge, must serve this purpose. And everything must be examined from this point of view and used to prevent white genocide and secure a homeland for our future generations. This we pledge.*

Outside the open window, the boys squatted, silent and astonished. The words being recited may not have been fully understood, but they all knew that this was a group of white supremacists, the kind they had heard about on CNN. Wally turned his head and looked at the others. "I think we need to get outta here!"

"No! I wanna hear what this guy is gonna say," Ed said insistently.

"Tonight is a grand night for us, my comrades, The Wasp has stung!" The audience broke the silence and began cheering. It appeared that they were celebrating some kind of victory. The boys were fixed on the white-haired leader. *Wonder what that means,* thought Wally as the leader's voice continued to echo throughout the hall.

"Many now are dead. Evil religions have propagated the extermination of the whites, those of us chosen by God. We had to flee Israel, travel to northern Europe, and then make our new homeland in America. Sacrifices were made by ancient Israelites, our ancestors. This migration gives us our birthright!! We are ancestors of the Assyrian conquest of the northern kingdom of Israel in the 8th century BCE. We are exiles of many, bringing our lineages to the United States and Canada. This is now our homeland. We must to protect it at all costs. The non-white tribes are invading and we are being slowly exterminated once again by the nonwhites and the liberals, like the ancient days in the Bible. Our fathers tried to stop this in the Forties; then they had government backing. What they now call The Greatest Generation tried to keep the inferior tribes in their place. The blacks were not given access to mortgages. True, the non-whites were forced to ghettos but at least they had someplace to live!! Now, because of leftwing liberals and their political funding, the tribes are moving to our neighborhoods. They call this diversity, claiming it will make America stronger. But the questions is for who? It's damn sure not for us white men. No, it's a slow process of taking our homeland!"

The boys heard one of the paramilitary soldiers sitting near the edge of an aisle say. "The niggers an' wetbacks ain't worth a f***, damn gov'ment and the f****** WOKE movement. Tryin' to take 'way what's been promised t' us by God!"

Wally noticed that the unshaven man had a flushed alcoholic face and it was hard to understand him between his slurred speech and southern drawl. Wally rolled his eyes and whispered, "What a discriminatory drunkard dirt bag." Looking at the bitter man, it was hard to tell where his mustache ended and his lip started. Meanwhile, up front, The Chicken Colonel continued.

"The establishment wants us weakened. This is a long-term miscegenation; they are brainwashing our children to mix with nonwhites. Look at the television! Look at the shows! Look at the commercials! Genetic pollution! Our daughters will be given to the Mexicans and blacks. We must stop the WOKE movement. Why did we let the non-white tribes loose? We are the pure and more intelligent race. Genetic studies show hard evidence, my WASP comrades. DNA studies show connections between European populations and the ancient Near East, including Israelites. To cite my claim! A study published in the journal Nature Communications in 2013 found genetic similarities between Ashkenazi Jews (a Jewish ethnic group with roots in Central and Eastern Europe) and Europeans. More proof that we are God's chosen!!" A huge cheer – more like a roar – bellowed from the followers. The leader, his face growing even redder, continued.

"Even some of our own women are subscribing to this invasion. They are aiding the white-genocide movement. They are choosing careers over child-bearing and being happy with bearing no more than two children. Men, two children per healthy household is not enough to preserve us. I mandate that each of you have three children; this will keep our race replacement value over two. Less than two we will give the WOKE movement what they want -- a slow death of the white race!"

A militant in the crowd shouted angrily. "That's right! Women should be home. Raising our offspring. I provide by driving my eighteen-wheeler! No lazy-ass Mexican will take my job! Put thar asses back ov'r the borda!" Another roar responded to his rant.

The colonel paused stroked his beard. "Even the white churches have fallen into the liberal trap. They say diversity will make American stronger. Blacks are filling the white churches. Not only that, the old traditional hymns are being replacement by black soul music. Other churches are allowing fags to be preachers. This is an abomination of the God's laws. Man shall not lie with another man! Whites shall not lie with non-whites! We must act now! We must stop the WOKE influence. 'Wokism' must be stopped. WASPs, it's our job to sting again!"

The men in the assembly stood on their feet cheering, "Sting! Sting! Sting! Defeat, Defeat, Defeat!"

Suddenly, Mike grabbed Dalton's shoulder and pointed, "Look! Over there -- a guard!" They saw a red light flash on the other side of the building. Their hearts had already started to pound hard in their chests, shocked by what they had just heard, but they all knew that getting caught by armed fanatics could be the end.

Ed hissed, "Guys, how are we getting out of here?!"

CHAPTER 24
IN A FLASH BACK TO THE YURT

A blinding flash of lighting hit the tallest fir tree in the compound, too close behind the boys. Inside, the entire company of men looked out the window above where the boys squatted. The loud thunder that followed – so close and so loud – made the moment even more frightening, causing their hearts to race even more than their fear of being caught by the WASP soldiers.

"We have got to *move!*" shouted Dalton, not worried about being heard above the thunder and the rising wind. The others were still trying to recover from their shock. At the moment, the boys were prisoners of the storm within this mysterious paramilitary compound and their fears of being caught by the guards who had no doubt been trained to secure the compound…and their intimidating red head lamps that cut through the darkness made escape seemingly impossible. The lightning strikes that lit up everything made things even more complicated.

The guards were moving towards their location quickly, most likely to investigate any damage generated by the strike. The boys' hopes burned like flickering flames, but they knew that if they wanted to taste freedom again, they must seize this moment and make a daring escape.

Quickly, together, the four boys devised a plan. Communicating their thoughts without a sound, all looked toward the safety of the perimeter fence. "The fence! We gotta make it to the fence!" Wally whispered, "The guards'll be going to check out the lightning strike. Use this as a distraction and move now!!" At that precise moment, a tremendous downpour followed yet another flash and boom. Relentless pelting rain drowned out any sound their footsteps made as they darted from shadow to shadow. The quick thinking allowed them to slip past the distracted guards, undetected as they were lost in the shadows of the compound buildings and sheets of blowing rain. Hunched over, they moved quickly to the dark area where the fence disappeared into the forest foliage. Breathing hard, hearts still racing, they dashed about fifty yards through red mud and wet grassy weeds. That snatched at their legs. In the lead, Dalton searched for a way out. *"God, please give us something!"* he thought desperately. Just then. as he looked to his left, he saw a dumpster in the darkness On his next step, he felt a depression and knew it had to be a path or a game trail worn by rats, opossums, and raccoons making their nocturnal visits to eat the troops' food scraps tossed into the open dumpster. Signaling, Dalton dashed right along the shallow ditch and moved toward the fence hurriedly. At the base of the fence, just as he hoped, he saw a small hole dug by the scavenging mammals.

Dalton began scooping the red mud from the potential escape hole; the others joined him. Wally and Ed, digging side by side, felt something hard and large. Wally said, "It's a big freakin' rock!" Dalton shouted, "Hurry up, dig it out!" Mike joined in the effort and all three rolled the large stone and flipped it over and out of the way. Once clear, the boys scrambled through the hole and under the fence, conscious of voices shouting somewhere in the wet forest behind them. Ed, the largest of the four, scraped his back on the fence's jagged bottom and blood mixed with rain quickly appeared on his flannel shirt. He got to the safety outside the fence and quickly turned and lifted the wire for the others to pass through easier.

Frantically, they crawled to the border of the woods, their bellies and arms pricked by wild rose thorns and blackberry vines. Fighting against pain, they were finally able to use clumps of small pine and hardwood saplings for cover. Once in the safety of the lower forest canopy, they jumped to their feet and sprinted through the darkness. Finally, the boys reached the base of the cliff and knew the safety of the yurt was a few hundred yards away. With as much energy they could muster, driven by pure, fear-driven adrenaline and groping for handholds, they scaled the cliff made their way to the security of the campsite and the fire pit.

Dalton, collapsing next to the yurt and gasping for breath, began to laugh, "That was awesome!" Ed, equally winded, still trembled with fear. Dalton's light brown hair clung to his forehead as he shook his head, sending water droplets scattering around him. "We're completely soaked," he exclaimed, the dampness evident in his voice. "Get those coals going agin."

"An' covered in mud!" laughed Wally as he and Mike got up, still breathing hard, changed out of their wet clothes.

Each reached for their water bottles and took gigantic gulps. The water leaked passed Wally's lips. Moving his bottle just below his chin, he said, "Can you believe that? Did you listen to that bastard's words? I have never heard such open bigotry like that!"

"Women, wetbacks and niggers. Who talks like that?!" Mike sneered.

"He claims his Biblical lineage is pure. Bullshit. He broke every red letter in the Bible in those ten minutes," Wally continued. He doesn't even know what WOKE means. What the hell do they think WOKISM is? These bastards have perverted and weaponized it! The true meaning is *being aware of your political choice and social justice.* First occurred in the lyrics of a 1938 song by the blues singer Lead Belly," Wally added, looking at the others, His song about the Scottsboro Boys, nine black teenagers wrongly accused of rape and sentenced to death, warns of the dangers of a racially prejudiced justice system and concludes *"best stay woke."* In other words, *you better watch your back.* The right wingers have turned it into a racial slur. It was never meant to be that. Those assholes need to find a better word for their agenda to erase the non-whites. Pitilessly prejudice punks and following ideas made by Hitler himself."

Ed questioned, "But why do they attack religion?"

Mike countered, "Well, it sure don't seem like the Jesus I follow. *"Fags as preachers?"* Sin is sin and those white boys are sure as hell are not free of it. What makes them think they can be judge jury and executioner? Whites are more intelligent than the nonwhites? Bullshit. How about George Washington Carver? I bet most all of them ate peanut butter this month. In terms of talent and skills, maybe they had their way before the nineteen fifties-no Hank Aaron, no Michael Jordan, and *no* Martin Luther King.

Dalton said, "Country music and rock would suck today if it were not for the blacks' influence. They are xenophobic white trash."

Wally suddenly blurted out loud, "Hey. What did Colonel Chicken mean by, sting?"

Meanwhile, no one seemed to have noticed when the rain had stopped washing their mud off. The only sound, after all the cracking and sizzling of the lightning and the booming of thunder, was the steady dripping from the trees around and above them.

CHAPTER 25
MARTIN LUTHER KING STATUE
UNDER THE MATTRESS

Sirens blaring five black Chevrolet suburban's followed two Sherriff patrol cars. They entered the middle class subdivision in Raleigh North Carolina. Flashed the search warrant to the guard at the front gate. The guard did a thumbs up and manually opened the barrier gate. After passing through the guard at the gate; they accelerated into the narrow streets. Players on the tennis courts and basketball court stopped and watched the convoy pass. A child from the nearby playground ran to her mom on the tennis court, scared and crying, reached out with her arms and mom gathered her up and said, "Honey it's okay." The peaceful community had changed into a mission-capture the person or persons that poisoned the innocent people in the churches.

"Washington's house is on a cul de sac, 13 Spider Ridge Lane."

Walesy ordered into his shoulder communication device as he rode in the passenger of the lead black suburban. The group of law enforcement vehicles took an immediate right turn and filled the entire space in the cul de sac. All vehicles faced the front of the house. Four officers went directly to the backyard. From his shoulder mic, "keep your head on a swivel!" Ordered Dr. Walesy.

As they jumped out their cars, Holland said, "The house is a twostory structure with three bedrooms. First floor is an open floor plan. Move slowly and scan all parts of the house. Who knows what we are rushing into?" The team worked in pairs and move strategically around each blind corner and opening closet doors. Through the mikes, Holland said, "upstairs clear"… Walesy said, "Downstairs clear…" Hey Allen, whatta bout the backyard, what's the assessment?" asked Walesy

Allen with three deputies stated. "Detached garage is clear and no vehicle. The garage door is open." Standing in front of a wall-sized picture of Robert E. Lee, Walesy ordered, "Search everything. We are searching for anything that ties him to extremist group. Concentrating on the downstairs the team searched the study and the kitchen first. Each person moved swiftly and looked under furniture, rugs and pulled drawers and opened closets; nothing was left unturned.

"Hey we found a hidden compartment within desk drawer!"

"Where are you?" asked Walesy. "Open in up!

"We're in the study! I'm trying!" Holland spoke into her shoulder mic.

As Walesy rushed to the study, he heard one of deputies say, "Got it opened!" Holland gathered all the papers and started shuffling through the stack. As she looked at each one she laid them on the desk. In the stack was a map of the National Forest in Virginia. A small old logging camp was circled. It was near a river and the only markings on the map were horse trails and wilderness camp sites. "Sir, stuffed under his mattress is a picture of Martin Luther King's statue in Atlanta. Also, there's a map showing all the buildings surrounding the statue."

"Why?"

"Those bastards could be planning on blowing it up!"

"FBI picked up some chatter about retaliation. It might be a retaliation for the Robert E. Lee statue and the other confederate monuments removed all over the Southeast US."

"How do ya know that?"

"I don't for sure but, Jesus, can you imagine? If he's successful, ther's gonna be riots in every major city."

"That's jumpin to a conclusion! We need more evidence."

"Keep looking!" Ordered Walesy

The collection of gun magazines on his living room coffee table indicated his interest in firearms and increased the concerns about his intentions. Under the magazines was the Charlottesville Daily Progress newspaper dated May 15, 2017. Front page entitled the Day of Death. The article detailed *Alt Rights* protest of the Robert E. Lee statue removal in Downtown Park Charlottesville VA. "This is it! He's part of the white supremacy movement. It's starting to connect! He killed Steve Turner or knows who took the shot." At this moment a lifted Ford 150 turned onto Spider Ridge Lane. Its breaks screeched; the tires in reverse threw black smoke; sped off down the narrow street of the subdivision. All officers ran to their cars. Drivers pressed the gas pedals and the engines roared after the Ford Truck. The officers in the passenger seat called in the chase to dispatch. All law enforcement agencies began a manhunt to capture Michael Washington. The dragnet covered the entire Raleigh metropolitan area. Michael Washington did not get far. He tried to get onto I-440, the Raleigh Beltline. Five state troopers formed a blockade across the ramp. All officers were behind their patrol cars and armed; they pointed pistols and rifles at his truck. Michael Washington tried to go into reverse, however the black suburban pulled behind him. He had no way out. He lifted his arms and showed his palms through the windshield.

"Why do you have a picture of Martin Luther King's Statue?" Are you going to blow it up?"

In full denial, "NO!"

Walesy fired back. "My team has facial recognition evidence that you were at the Charlottesville riot in 2017 and we have you also at J-6. You are affiliated with the Alt Right; you're not alone! Your fanatic friends are responsible for the churches, and I think you're about to do something drastic. I'm calling this domestic terrorism.

Send him to Guantanamo Bay. Let the real interrogation begin. Water board this sonna bitch!!

Holland interrupted and said "WASP!" The strategy was planned to see a reaction and Washington turned away from Walesy. He looked directly at Holland. "Yeah! I thought so."

Walesy leaned forward inches from Washington's face. "You recognized that name, don't you? I saw it in your body language. That's your boys, huh? Are you and your vigilante friends pissed about ol Robert E. Lee having a meltdown. Maybe they'll make a bronze statue of Claudette Colvin. Ya know she would not give up the bus seat before Rosa Parks. Yes she was the first!" Walesy laughed out loud with a satirical ha ha ha. Michael Washington grimaced. In a flash Holland reached into a folder and slammed the National Forest Map in front of Washington.

Holland was inches from Washington's ear, "Why's this old abandoned saw mill circled?"

CHAPTER 26
AGENTS AND COWBOYS

Walesy and Holland stepped out of the interrogation room. Michael Washington sat solitarily; very fidgety, and Allen watched from the one way window. Walesy and Holland moved into the conference room across the hallway.

Holland poured a cup of coffee and sat down across from Walesy. Holland said, "Boss what should we do next?"

"Let me think on it. I'm not really sure yet." Walesy put his index finger on his lips.

After a few minutes Allen stepped into the conference room. "This guy, Washington, is very anxious. He's gotta know the next attack!" Walesy after a pause, rubbed his forehead. "We don't have time to get information on the next attack outta him. We must act on the information we have. Contact Atlanta FBI, and tell them to send a unit to observe the area around the Martin Luther King statue. The statue must be protected; it's symbol is essential to the United States to move forward for peaceful democracy. These home grown terrorists – WASP- whatever they call themselves are trying to make a societal statement. If these assholes are successful, it will set racism in the US back 40 years! We cannot allow this to happen. We have to get to the logging camp. Call our jet pilot, wheels up in 30! Contact Langley, they must have a helicopter ready at Shenandoah Valley Regional. Then get someone that knows the fire road! We have got to get to the logging camp! Sherriff or Park Service, somebody."

The CIA agents exited their plane and looked for a military or police helicopter. All they saw was a blue and gold huey. Painted on the nose cone was a beautiful mountain landscape. Waiting at the airport was a pilot with his unruly white hair and handle bar mustache. His six foot frame stood confidently on the helipad, sporting a stylish leather flight jacket. He greeted the team, "Hey ya all looking for a lift?, get it, a lift," He made a strange face moving his lips above and below his teeth. With the slight tilt in his face, his facial expression resembled a donkey. Holland uneasy about his facial expression, avoided eye contact and peered at his chest. He wore a jacket that bore the marks of age and adventure. The age of the flight jacket matched the age of the huey. The helicopter's rotor blades began to spin, creating a rhythmic thump that echoed Walesy's heartbeat.

As the helicopter lifted off the ground, strange man's eyes gleamed with a mixture of curiosity and exhilaration. The wind tousled his flight jacket collar as he skillfully guided the aircraft to the Blue Ridge.

Walesy handed the coordinates to their bizarre pilot. The pilot pulled his hair from his eyes and lifted the paper to his nose, "38.392188 latitude and -78.7060068 longitude. Yea, that's the old loggin camp. There seems to be some activity around that dilapidated place I've noticed some trucks move in and out of that place, recently.

Beautiful Blue Ridge Mountains surrounded the Shenandoah Airport. As the chopper lifted off the runway the team could see the picturesque valley. The team peered out the windows looking at stunning landscapes and natural beauty of the Shenandoah Valley.

Holland, said "it looks so peaceful."

Walesy grabbed his stomach and the old huey lifted off. "Woah." He then reached for the handrail.

"Hey boss little too much roller coaster?" chuckled Allen.

"Dr. Walesy!" Ther's the camp. Do ya want to put ya down in that open space?"

"No! Don't put us down there. Too close! We do not want them alarmed. Drop us off at Massanutten Ski resort near the entrance to the horse trail! We will move in on foot. We do not want any of them to escape. I would think the men in the camp know the terrain and it would be hard to find all of the militants. I want every last one of them! We have got to catch them off guard!"

The huey dropped down in the large lot of the Massanutten Ski Resort. Walesy and his investigative team jumped from the sliding door. Leaves were swirling and the loose soil was making visibility difficult. Off in the distance about one hundred meters Walesy saw four horseman moving towards the landing site. As he watched two of the horses became very agitated by the sound of the chopper.

Mike patted his horse on the shoulder, "Woe baby!"

Dalton said, "What's gonnin on up there?" Just then the chopper took off and moved out of sight. Dalton said "stop! woah!" He released his heels and tightened up the reins. "Let's wait here. We don't know who they are." Mike's horse settled down as Mike reached over to give her a piece of apple.

Walsey looked at his team and then said. "Let's talk to the four on the horses. Maybe they have seen something."

Holland walked towards Wally, Dalton, Mike, and Ed. "Hey, young men, how are you doin? Have you been on this trail for a while?

Wally spoke up. "Yes mam. We've been out here for nine days."

"Wow, you cowboys have covered some ground. Where did you start?"

Dalton said boastfully, "Mam about fifty eight miles back. We'll cover sixty when we finish."

Walesy was curious but with a very stern and assertive face. The boys recognized quickly that he was a federal investigator. "Have you young men seen anything unusual?"

The boys turned towards each other eyes wide open each other. Ed said, "What do you mean, sir? Unusual?"

"Gentlemen, we are looking for a group of men who have done some very bad things. We believe they are responsible for the church poisonings and might be up to another attack on innocent people."

"You mean the WASP?" Wally identified. "Those men are evil. We heard some crazy stuff. We wanted to report it. You're the first law enforcement authority we have seen since listen'in to their meeting."

All the agents looked at each other with astonishment. "What do you mean meeting?" Holland with a puzzled look and eyes squinted.

Ed eagerly wanted to inform the agents, blurted, "They were ranting about being the God's people and that America was trying to get rid of their pure ancestry. They even used the word genocide. Kept calling minorities- tribes. It was some crazy stuff. Chosen people, their ancestors were from Northern Israel back in the ancient days."

Dalton added, "Yea… Said women should have three babies. Stay home an' cook." He looked at agents Allen and Holland. He rolled his eyes. "Boy, he's lucky mom didn't hear that stuff." Allen and Holland smiled.

Holland commented "sounds like your Mom raised you to be respectful."

"Yes Mam! Always."

"How many men?" Walesy demanded, cutting to the chase.

"Not sure, but it looked like a Duck Dynasty church service. And ther's this leader called Colonel Sanders. The boys laughed. Geez. Looked like chicken man himself. White goatee and the whole bit." The boys laughed again, and Walesy smirked at the description.

"We were there last night and almost got caught. We snuck in and walked past some military training equipment and a bunch of old buildings. You can see it for yourself Mister, just go back to the yurt and look over the cliff, you can see them. I think their getting ready to do something. We heard them say. WASP will sting agin. Not sure what that means." Wally announced.

CHAPTER 27
YEA RIGHT, NATURAL GAS EXPLOSION.

Inside the breakroom of the CDC sat Snider, Siribondu and Withers. Exhausted from the travel, investigation, and the laboratory research, they were taking a well needed break from the suits. They were in the early stages of the post epidemic protocol. Safe storage and recording of the toxic agents. Labels had to be accurate for future reference. The information is crucial to resolve future crisis. The greatest enemy in an epidemic is time. Preparedness is the best way to stop a threat. "Hey, Snider, I did't wear make up today," smiled Siribondu as she removed the final layer of the head protection. Her black had static and stood straight up. Withers thoughtfully looked at her and pushed her own hair down to make Siribondu aware. Siribondu quickly brushed her hands through her hair.

"Wonder, if Walesy caught the perpetrators yet? It's just unbelievable to me how some people have no regard for life." Withers pondered.

"I wish I knew," responded Snider.

"We did our part and I'm glad to be a part of this team." Siribondu said in a thankful tone and appreciative facial expression. Snider smiled and got up from his chair and reached to back of the refrigerator for a red Gatorade. As he moved back to sit at the table he picked up the TV remote. He pressed the power button and FOX news flashed on the screen. The network was covering a story in rural Virginia. A huge billowing gray cloud filled the entire sky behind the reporter. On the ground were fire trucks and hoses going in all directions. Firemen ran back and forth in the small camp. "Geez that place is so old let it burn." Snider commented.

"Wonder what that place is? It's so remote."

"Looks like an old abandoned logging camp." Withers was focused on the screen.

The reporter continued covering the story. I'm speaking to Massanutten Resort fire chief. "Sir, do we know the cause of the fire and are we concerned about it spreading into the National Forest?"

"Well to answer your first question, the forensic evidence seems to indicate that the natural gas line leaked and a spark of some kind ignited. The tank then exploded. Just like a very large bomb. A few men were here and all are dead. The initial blast we believe killed the majority. Well, others... Your second question.."

Snider pointed at the screen. "Look! Is that Walesy?"

"Where?"

"I think it is, why is he in a Forest Service Uniform?" questioned Withers.

"Huh, a natural gas explosion?" Snider looked suspicious as he made eye contact with the others...

CHAPTER 28
RAPTURE?

The Blue Ridge Mountains' majestic landscape surrounded the boys, the peaks reaching towards the heavens as the cowboys rode their mounts along The Massanutten Ridge Trail, the final leg of their journey. All were relieved that the long undertaking was nearing the end. The young men's rendezvous point with Dalton's grandfather was at the parking lot of General Store near the Massanutten Resort ski slopes. From their panoramic viewpoint, the boys could see thick, billowing clouds of dark grey rolling across the sky, gradually obscuring the vibrant blue that once was dominated by huge puffy white cumulous clouds which were disappearing quickly. A sense of anticipation hung in the air as the atmosphere grew heavy with humidity. The distant rumble of thunder echoed through the valley, setting the stage for the arrival of nature's spiritual symphony. "Durn, we're in for a big one! Get the ponchos!" Ed yelled. The soon-to-be-soaked trail ended at a wide path that the high traffic volume of both day hikers and equestrians had worn. Nearing the end there was one more challenge; the boy's horses were traversing large granite outcroppings. Mike and Wally were relieved to see the cell phone tower on top of the highest peak. Fewer than a hundred feet away from the trail sat a metal hang-gliding ramp. Standing on it. Two sky-surfers were about to glide to the valley below.

Ed looked briefly at the edge and said, "It's insane to think of people just running and jumping offa that, especially with those black clouds an' lightning in the distance!"

His companions were silent; tired, thirsty and foul-smelling; none of them had taken a shower for a few days. Being in the same condition, they didn't sense each other's body odors, but a young girl, around ten, standing in the path with her family, said, innocently, as the boys passed, "Daddy, those boys smell worse than the horses!"

Embarrassed, the mother avoided eye contact with the boys but said loudly, "Honey, that's not a very nice thing to say."

The father quickly responded to ease the awkwardness, "Long ride, boys?"

Proudly, Dalton responded with a tired smile, "Two weeks, sir, out in the wild."

"Well, that's quite a challenge for young men such as yourselves… for anyone, as a matter of fact! I'm sure you've been making lifetime memories." Hearing that, they all found a little energy left to sit taller in their saddles.

"Hey, guys, we're almost where we're supposed to meet Granddad. He's gonna be in the general store parking lot," Dalton called as he passed the young family, giving his horse a small pat. The horses seemed to show signs of the same fatigue that the boys were feeling. Sweat was running from the horses' shoulders and flanks; froth was slowly starting to build around their dry lips.

"Hey, Dalton, old Silver needs a drink. Should we stop?" Mike called.

Wally replied, "Only a half mile left. We'll take care of them when we dismount and pull the tack!"

Dalton agreed. "Guys, we don't wanna make granddad wait. Push on!" He gave his horse a kick and the rest followed.

The rumbling of passing cars from somewhere below was getting louder and louder. Soon, in the distance, the boys could see tourists dashing across the parking lot to the general store.

Finally, Mike said with a groan in obvious relief, "How long is it gonna take for my butt to recover?"

Dalton laughed, "You can stand in the horse trailer with the horses on the trip back home."

"And you can stay in there with me and rub it, Dalton!" Mike retorted. Ed chuckled with his fist over his mouth.

Arriving at the general store, the young men dismounted and pulled the saddles off the horses, and tied the horses to one of the hitching posts in front of large storage lockers, each that was large enough to provide room for a horse blanket, saddle and bridle. Placed directly beside the posts was a trough with an old-fashioned well pump. Each young man took turns pumping the long metal handle until fresh mountain water poured out in a thick stream. Eagerly, the horses plunged their mouths into the water and drank. Even with the horses' lips below the surfaced of the water, the boys could hear the horses slurping as their throats pulsed as they swallowed. Mike patted old Silver and said, "There girl, good girl," as he stroked her mane and moved his hand down her muscular body to wipe the sweat from her shiny white coat.

At the same time, Dalton's grandfather was turning right onto Mountain View Drive. Flickers of lightning in the clouds illuminated the darkened sky. Powerful bolts streaked across the heavens, dancing among the mountain peaks, creating a breathtaking display against the inky backdrop formed by the ominous cumulonimbus clouds. Within minutes, those clouds opened up with a tremendous downpour as the grandfather arrived at the general store parking lot, windshield wipers on high; outside the comfort of the heavy-duty truck, the rain continued to pour, as if it were a battle between nature and machine, and the wipers were barely enough to provide clear visibility. Dalton's granddad, eager and excited to see the boys waved to some people under the store's overhanging roof that he assumed were his grandson's friends.

As he had done many times before, he swung his big rig's trailer entry ramp close to the tied-up horses. After setting his emergency brake, he looked in his large side-view mirror, covered with streams of rainwater to confirm his position for an easy load. The elderly grayhaired man slid across the soft leather seat of his Ford Lariat truck and stepped out onto the parking lot. Astonishing, the pouring rain stopped in an instant as he felt the warm sunshine on his somewhat wet back. Looking up, he watched a moment of pure magic unfold as a perfect rainbow painted the sky with all seven colors. Against the backdrop of the quickly fading storm, sunlight burst through the remaining raindrops, crafting a masterpiece that seemed too beautiful to be real. As he walked back to the large horse trailer, he inspected the tires. Then he again noticed the boys' horses and tack…but the boys he had waved to as he entered the parking lot had vanished. Turning, he shouted, "Dalton, hey, you cowboys, where are you?!" Then he changed his focus to the hitching posts and saw the boys' clothes on the ground by the horses…but saw no trace of the boys.